Developing Leadership Teams
in the Bivocational Church

Dr. Terry W. Dorsett

CROSSBOOKS
PUBLISHING

CrossBooks™
A Division of LifeWay
1663 Liberty Drive
Bloomington, IN 47403
www.crossbooks.com
Phone: 1-866-879-0502

First published by CrossBooks 7/22/2010

ISBN: 978-1-6150-7252-1 (sc)

Library of Congress Control Number: 2010908261

Printed in the United States of America
Bloomington, Indiana

This book is printed on acid-free paper.

I would like to express my appreciation to:

My professors at Golden Gate Baptist Theological Seminary, who pushed me to publish this work.

The pastors and lay leaders of the Green Mountain Baptist Association, who spent months helping me test out the teaching sessions that make up the last six chapters of this book.

Mr. and Mrs. Jim Arrington and Mrs. Charlotte Hoover, who invested significantly in my education and in the development of these materials.

Georgia Herod, Rita Beall and Sarah Killough, who spent countless hours proof-reading this document and helping ensure a good flow of thought from chapter to chapter.

My wonderful family, who allowed me to have many quiet hours away from them to write, re-write, edit and produce this work. I could never have done this without the support of my wife Kay, and my three children, Katie, Taylor and Jonas.

Contents

Chapter 1

Small Church Realities

Tom's Story

Tom graduated seminary full of passion and enthusiasm for using his faith to make a difference in the world around him. He and his young wife were so excited when a small church near his hometown called him as pastor. Their commitment to making a significant difference in their community through their church caused them to throw themselves into as many activities as they could. Like many small churches, Tom's church was not able to fully-fund his salary, so he worked a second job at a local business to help support his family. At first the excitement of it all kept Tom energized and passionate about his new role as the pastor of a small church. But as time went by, the pressure of raising a family, caring for the needs of the church and working a second job to help pay for it began to have a negative impact in Tom's life. As the pressure began to build, Tom began to lose his excitement and energy for ministry. He tried to pray more in order to regain his passion, but he was often so exhausted that he would fall asleep during his prayer time. His wife tried to help all that she could, but with two small children at home and her part-time Internet business, her time also had great demands on it. Tom began to have anxiety attacks. His blood pressure rose to unhealthy levels. His wife would often gently remind him of how long it had been since he had been home for dinner with the family. Finally, four years into what Tom thought was going to be a lifelong adventure, Tom resigned from the church and moved his family to a larger community where he took a full time job teaching at the local community college. When friends and family asked Tom if he was ever going to re-enter the ministry, he would respond that he did not want to talk about it.

Every year godly pastors such as Tom, who serve small churches that are unable to fully support their salary, leave the ministry. Some of these pastors will eventually re-enter the ministry, but many will never return to a calling they once found so fulfilling. Such pastors are often referred to as bivocational pastors because they have two vocations, one that is ministry oriented and another that is outside the church. While there are many reasons why bivocational pastors may leave the ministry, a significant one is that they simply burn-out. The pressures of working secular jobs and carrying on the duties of leading churches become too great for some bivocational pastors to bear. When these pastors leave

1

the ministry, the churches are deprived of their experience, their passion, and their unique gifts and talents. Churches cannot afford to continue to lose so many good leaders.

Bivocational pastors face not only the additional pressure of working a second job to support their ministry; they also must frequently deal with a perceived second-class status in ministry. Over time, this perception of bivocational ministry being second-class has resulted in a negative social stigma being attached to the concept of bivocational ministry. Some pastors feel a sense of inadequacy when serving in bivocational roles. They may not even want to think of themselves as bivocational because of the perceived stigma attached to the term.

The negative stigma that is often attached to bivocational ministry has led to some debate over what actually defines bivocational pastors. Dennis Bickers, who has written numerous books on bivocational ministry, believes that the term is rightly used to describe "one who has a secular job as well as a paid ministry position in a church."[1]

Doran McCarty served as a professor at a well regarded seminary and is a recognized educator of bivocational ministers. McCarty defines bivocational ministers as "persons who serve more than one vocation or institution and/or whose income is partly derived from some other source than the institutions of their primary religious employment."[2] These two writers agree with many others who define the term "bivocational" in connection to ministers who receive income from and/or hold employment outside the church.

Many types of bivocational pastors exist. Some are only working part-time jobs outside the church to supplement their ministry incomes. Others receive a majority of their income from outside the churches they serve. Others have private sources of income without which they would be unable to accomplish the ministry to which they have been called. But all those ministers who would be unable to serve their churches without these various streams of outside income are correctly defined as bivocational pastors.

It is important to note that bivocational pastors must actually be working for churches in a vocational way in order to be considered bivocational. Bivocational pastors are not just a higher class of volunteers. They are actually employed by churches to do some type of ministry. The Southern Baptist Bivocational Minister's Association notes that however small it may be, "some financial support for the church-related responsibility constitutes bivocational, as distinguished from volunteer."[3] While numerous individuals serve churches in a wide variety of ways as volunteers, they would not be considered bivocational ministers.

Due to a lack of understanding, people will occasionally refer to bivocational pastors as part-time pastors, a misnomer because all pastors are on call twenty-four hours a day. Therefore, there are no actual part-time pastors. When discussing this issue, Dennis Bickers suggests "rather than referring to full-time or part-time ministers, it is much better to call ministers either fully-funded or bivocational."[4]

While there may be no part-time pastors, there are situations in which full-time ministers must discover income from other sources so they can accomplish the ministry to which they have been called. Ronald Hornecker and Doran McCarty write in their book *Making the Most of Change* that "it is more accurate to talk of bivocational churches than bivocational pastors."[5] This is probably a more accurate way to describe bivocational ministry.

Regardless of whether the term "bivocational" is used to describe the pastors or the churches they serve, many denominations and their various institutions, agencies, and theological educational programs have routinely neglected the unique needs of bivocational pastors and the churches they serve. This neglect may have been unintentional. Nevertheless, it sends a subtle message about the perceived value of bivocational pastors. This trend of neglect must be reversed.

Some denominations and their related organizations are beginning to understand the seriousness of the need to offer encouragement and support to bivocational pastors. Steve Nerger, former National Missionary for Bivocational Ministry for the North American Mission Board of the Southern Baptist Convention, has led that denomination in using bivocational ministers for church planting. With excitement he declares that "bivocationalism is now seen as a strategy in building the core of a new church."[6] The decision to move bivocational pastors into the mainstream of that denomination's church planting strategy has also led to greater training, encouragement, and support of those pastors.

Bivocational ministry is not the right decision for all pastors and all churches. Dennis Bickers reminds his readers that "the call to bivocational ministry is a call to a specific ministry for both the church and the minister, and how blessed when both respond to this call with joy and anticipation that God is going to do something powerful as a result."[7] Bivocational ministry is not the place for those whose ministry skills are so inadequate that they cannot find a fully-funded church to serve. There are also some ministry situations where the ministry needs are such that only a fully-funded pastor will be effective. But the reality is that bivocational pastors have been and will continue to be a significant part of the leadership in many of America's churches. Therefore, churches and the agencies that serve them must find ways to assist bivocational pastors in being as effective and healthy as possible.

One Example of the Importance of Bivocational Ministry

Bivocational ministers are clearly in the mainstream of Southern Baptist Convention efforts in Vermont. According to materials produced by that denomination's Executive Committee, Vermont was the last state where Southern Baptists established a ministry presence.[8] Baptist historian Merwyn Borders recalls the story of how Roscoe and Daisy Anderson began Southern Baptist ministry in Vermont in 1963 when they moved to Vermont as a result of Anderson's employment at the General Electric plant in South Burlington.[9] Though the Andersons were lay people, they felt a missionary calling to start a church. They were successful in their missionary endeavors and eventually the church they started was able to begin several other small missions across the state.

The Green Mountain Baptist Association was formed in 1982 to help that fledgling group of Southern Baptist churches and missions work together more effectively. Since its founding, the association has grown from a handful of struggling churches scattered across Vermont to thirty-seven churches and missions strategically located across the state.

Though the association has experienced significant growth in the number of churches, many of the individual churches within the association continue to be quite small. Southern Baptist Directory Services reports that in 2007 the median number of members per church was twenty-eight. In that same year, the median number of people attending worship at these churches on Sunday mornings was forty.[10] Due to these small numbers, bivocational pastors lead a significant portion of these churches.

As Southern Baptist churches across Vermont mature, some of them will grow and be able to support fully-funded pastors. However, a number of factors contribute to the reality that many of these churches will remain small. One of those factors is that according to December 2009 survey published in the *USA Today* newspaper, Vermont is the least religious state in America.[11] This lack of church connection in Vermont culture results in a larger number of smaller churches across the state than in most other parts of the nation.

Researcher Sybil McShane's report on literacy in rural areas reveals another factor that keeps churches in Vermont small, which is that Vermont is the most rural state in America.[12] Rural areas have lower population densities than more urban areas. This overall lack of population means that churches serving rural communities will typically have fewer attendees. Though churches in any community can grow, those that are in rural communities naturally do not have the potential to grow as large as those in more populous areas.

These factors combine to create an environment that is likely to keep most churches in the Green Mountain Baptist Association relatively small. One result of the small size of the churches is that bivocational pastors will continue to serve many of these churches. It is unrealistic to expect small churches to fully-fund pastors, no matter how well loved or deserving those pastors may be. Since bivocational ministry is the cultural reality of the association, the association has begun to more adequately meet the needs of bivocational pastors. This book grew out of the desire to help bivocational pastors in Vermont continue to be effective in ministry and avoid burn-out.

A significant issue that many bivocational pastors face is burn-out. When pastors become emotionally drained, this becomes a serious obstacle for smaller churches to overcome. While larger churches often have access to resources to help their pastors return to health, smaller churches rarely have that capability. When bivocational pastors become overloaded by constant pressure, they usually end up leaving the churches they serve. These frequent gaps in pastoral leadership cause the churches to struggle constantly to achieve health. Therefore, bivocational pastors must be assisted in their current ministry situations so they will not become exhausted and leave. As these pastors are assisted, they will have more energy to devote to ministry and will find greater fulfillment in their ministries. These pastors will also be able to remain in their churches longer, resulting in healthier churches and healthier pastors.

There is a Solution!

The purpose of this book is to assist pastors serving small churches that may not be able to fully-fund their salaries. The principles found in this book will assist pastors in creating pastoral leadership teams by equipping selected individuals to share in the preaching and pastoral care ministries of the local church. To clarify this purpose, several aspects of the above statement should be defined and understood.

Though this book was intended for bivocational pastors, it will also be of assistance to pastors of small churches even if they are not currently bivocational. Though some pastors in small churches may not actually be bivocational because they have some other means of support, such as a pension or trust fund, bivocational pastors will most likely serve those churches in the future. Therefore even pastors from small churches who are not technically bivocational will still benefit from this book because they will be able to use it to train the congregation to be more effective when the church does call a bivocational pastor at some point.

The goal of this book is to help these pastors develop pastoral leadership teams so that they are not doing the entire ministry themselves. Dr. Melvin Steinbron writes extensively on lay involvement in churches and he emphasizes that "the lay people must have personal ownership of the ministry and ownership comes from facing the need and developing the ministry together."[13] Only by working in partnership together can pastoral leadership teams help develop healthier churches and healthier pastors. By developing these teams, bivocational pastors will not be as prone to burn-out. Churches will also benefit from the development of these teams because they will have a multiple leadership approach instead of a single leader approach. A single leader approach leads to blaming the solo leader when things do not go as well as expected. A team leadership approach helps to avoid blaming one person for results that the individual leader had very little control over. Roy and Jackie Trueblood have led a training program for many years that helps laity and clergy partner together in ministry. They have also written extensively about this subject. They say that "an effective team is composed of members who take full responsibility for the results that are produced by the team and refuse to be seduced into blaming and justifying behavior."[14]

A key component to helping these pastors develop pastoral ministry teams will be to assist them in equipping selected individuals from their churches to aid them in their ministries. Not all people in every church will be able to serve on these pastoral leadership teams. Some will lack the desire, the spiritual commitment, or the skills needed to serve effectively on pastoral leadership teams. But those individuals that have the desire and the ability to serve on such teams will help their churches be effective even though their pastors may have limited time due to outside employment.

Once the pastors select these people, the people will need to be equipped. These people cannot be expected to serve without training and development. Therefore, a significant portion of the book will focus on helping the pastors train the individuals who have been selected to assist them. While there are many different ways pastoral leadership teams might work together, this book shall focus on equipping the teams for preaching and pastoral care ministries. These two aspects have been chosen because they are often the two most time-consuming components of pastoral ministry. If the pastors can share these two significant ministry burdens with their teams, they will be relieved from significant pressure. That, in turn, will make these pastors less likely to experience burn-out and more likely to be fulfilled in their ministry leadership. It will also help the lay people appreciate the stress level and demands that such ministry places on pastors.

Chapter 2

Biblical Principles To Consider

Building effective pastoral leadership teams requires having a good working knowledge of the theology of church leadership. Attempts to build these teams based solely on human organizational principles or modern business methodology will be inadequate in properly preparing people to work together in the spiritual dynamic of a local church. Several aspects of the theology of church leadership need to be considered in order to build a proper foundation for effective implementation of these ideas.

Bivocational Ministry Is Normative for the Church

The New Testament reflects bivocational ministry as normative for the church. Modern church attendees have come to expect pastors to devote all of their time to the ministries of the church. As a result, many modern church attendees do not understand that New Testament churches were often led by bivocational pastors. This misunderstanding has created unrealistic expectations for bivocational pastors because of their additional employment outside the church. If bivocational pastors are going to lead their churches effectively, they will first have to educate their congregations in how New Testament churches were led. The members of the churches must understand that it is normal to have pastors who work additional jobs and are unable to be involved personally in every aspect of the churches they serve. These members need to realize that having bivocational pastors was actually the New Testament norm instead of the exception.

A number of scriptures affirm the normalcy of bivocational ministry. The most well known New Testament examples of bivocational ministry come from the life of the Apostle Paul. Ron Rice, a bivocational pastor and denominational leader within the Colorado Baptist Convention, points out that "Paul shifted back and forth into the secular workforce at various times in his ministry career."[15] This makes him an excellent example of both fully-funded and bivocational ministry. It should also remove any negative stigma from the minds of those who think that bivocational ministry is somehow less honorable than fully-funded ministry. According to Dennis Bickers, Paul's ability to earn a living at something other than religious work "would have been in accordance with the practice of rabbis in Paul's time who believed that every rabbi must practice some trade to support himself."[16]

Luke records one of Paul's bivocational experiences in Acts 18:1-4:

> After this Paul left Athens and went to Corinth. And he found a Jew named Aquila, a native of Pontus, recently come from Italy with his wife Priscilla, because Claudius had commanded all the Jews to leave Rome. And he went to see them, and because he was of the same trade he stayed with them and worked, for they were tentmakers by trade. And he reasoned in the synagogue every Sabbath, and tried to persuade Jews and Greeks. (ESV)[17]

This passage indicates that Paul was a tentmaker. This was not just something that Paul did before he went into the ministry, but a vocation he was currently involved in while he was also in the process of ministry. The word for "tentmaker" (*skenopoios*) used here actually refers to leather working. Renowned New Testament scholar F. F. Bruce states: "This trade was closely connected with the principal product of Paul's native province, a cloth of goats' hair called cilicium, used for cloaks, curtains, and other fabrics designed to give protection against wet" conditions that were common to the area.[18] When Paul came to minister in Corinth, he met Aquila and Priscilla, who practiced the same trade. They apparently entered into some kind of business arrangement and worked together in their trade. The passage indicates that he also stayed with them, apparently in their home. Paul worked his trade during the week and then on the Sabbath he would go to the synagogue to persuade people to become followers of Jesus.

Paul's efforts to persuade people to become followers of Jesus in the synagogue were not just casual conversations he was having with individuals after the synagogue gathering. Darrell Bock, an expert on the book of Acts, points out that the word *reasoned* comes from the Greek word *dialegomia*, which "refers to either giving a discourse or to debating, depending on the context. Its combination with the next verb suggests debate in the synagogue."[19] Each Sabbath, Paul was having intense debates which were designed to convince people of the truth that Jesus was the Messiah. This would have required much thought and preparation. Paul found time for this preparation in addition to working in his trade as a tentmaker. Bivocational pastors must be good stewards of their time in order to prepare sermons and also work at their secular jobs. Dennis Bickers, who has served effectively in bivocational ministry for over thirty years, said it best when he declared, "Preaching is hard work, but it is also rewarding work. It takes a great deal of commitment to develop and present sermons each week, but your people deserve your very best effort in the pulpit."[20] Every bivocational pastor has experienced the truth of those words.

A second example of Paul's bivocational status is found in 1 Thess. 2:9. "For you remember our labor and hardship, brothers. Working night and day so that we would not burden any of you, we preached God's gospel to you." (HCSV)[21] In writing to the church of Thessalonica, Paul reminded them of his bivocational status while he served them. This was not new information to the church. Noted Pauline scholar Gene Green states they could "remember the manual labor that occupied Paul and his associates during their stay in the city."[22] Paul reminds them of the example that was set before them of working long hours while also preaching the gospel. Paul used the term "labor," which Green points out "most likely refers to any kind of self-sacrificing" work for the benefit of others.[23] Bivocational ministry is truly a labor of love that benefits the church. Gene goes on to say that the word *labor* "could denote 'trouble' or 'difficulty' but here the focus is on the type of work that results in fatigue and exhaustion."[24] Bivocational ministry is often exhausting. The demands of working two jobs are both physically and emotionally exhausting.

A third example of Paul's bivocational ministry is found in 2 Thess. 3:7-9:

> For you know that you ought to imitate us. We were not idle when we were with you. We never accepted food from anyone without paying for it. We worked hard day and night so we would not be a burden to any of you. We certainly had the right to ask you to feed us, but we wanted to give you an example to follow. (NLT)[25]

Paul again reminded the Thessalonians what they already knew, which was his past experience of bivocational ministry among them. Gene Green states that this repetitive reminder was "a well-known practice in ancient instruction."[26] It helped the learners recall what their teachers had previously taught them and also prepared them for further instruction.

The Thessalonians were being told to recall from Paul's example the importance of work. Having meaningful work was important because otherwise a person would become idle, which in turn would lead the individual into trouble.[27] Paul and his companions reminded the readers that while they were with them they worked hard and were not idle. Scholar Gene Green helps this verse become clearer when he writes; "The word translated 'to be idle' (*etaktesamen*) is the verbal form of the adverb 'disorderly' in 1 Thessalonians 5:14. The word means 'to be undisciplined' or 'to live in a disorderly manner' and is used to describe those who do not fulfill their obligations."[28] Paul and his companions were not disorderly. They were quite disciplined in their efforts both to earn a living and in preaching the gospel. Paul tells his readers to learn from his example of work. Likewise bivocational pastors and their ministry teams will need to remember that hard work is a good thing. They will be following in Paul's footsteps as they engage in the hard work of bivocational ministry.

Paul points out that they could have asked to be compensated adequately, but chose not to. It is important to note that many bivocational pastors could serve larger churches where they could be fully-funded in their ministry. But like Paul, they choose to serve in such as way as to not be a burden to anyone.

These passages demonstrate that bivocational ministry was normal in the New Testament. But it was also normal in American church life until fairly recently. James Greene, who helps train bivocational pastors through the North Carolina Baptist Convention, reminds churches that "the fact is that ministry in the early days of this country in the free church was bivocational. The term was not used because the style was the norm."[29] Since bivocational ministry was so common, no one thought to give it a name or define it. This was simply how ministers survived in the early days of American life. Dennis Bickers laments that despite the historical record, "some believe that bivocational ministry is something new, but it is actually the way most ministers served until fairly recently."[30] The transition away from bivocational ministry came as a result of the desire of churches to have a more educated clergy. James Greene explains that "in an attempt to raise the educational level of our ministerial leadership, churches and denominations in this country established a number of colleges and seminaries. Professionalism came with education."[31] Though all ministers should strive to be professionals, seminary education alone is not a guarantee of such behavior. This is especially true if an individual's call to ministry came later in life and that person is already a professional in another field. Attending seminary is not likely to make such a person more professional than he already is. Luther Dorr addressed this issue in his classic work, *The Bivocational Pastor:*

> Training for the church work is usually through formal education, such as seminary. But in many denominations the largest percentage of its ministers have been unable

to attend seminary. These people are doing great work because they have trained themselves through experience and informal opportunities of personal study. Many kinds of opportunities are available for ministers in any kind of situation.[32]

Dorr acknowledges that there are many pastors who may not have a seminary education but are still doing great work because of their experience and personal study. Regrettably Dorr also acknowledges that "some churches will not ordain a minister until he has completed his college and seminary education."[33] Many churches now falsely believe that a professionally trained and fully-funded clergy has always been a significant part of church life from the New Testament era until now. History simply proves that idea to be incorrect. Bivocational pastors will need to teach their churches a correct New Testament theology of church leadership and a correct history of church leadership in North American church life.

Shared Pastoral Leadership Is Normative for the Church

The New Testament demonstrates a shared pastoral leadership model as normative for the church. In modern times, many North American Protestant churches have become accustomed to a single-pastor model of church leadership. Researcher George Barna has discovered that "seven out of ten churches have a single paid professional, the pastor."[34] This model puts pastors in situations where they are serving alone as the primary leaders of the church. Not all these pastors are fully-funded, but they are seen as the primary leaders. In larger churches this model may be modified if there is a staff of pastors who serve under a senior pastor, but the basic concept is still that the senior pastor has a great deal of authority over the church. This single pastor model is especially evident in the preaching and pastoral care ministries of the church. The solo pastor, or the senior pastor in a larger church, is often expected to do almost all of the preaching and pastoral care.

When the bulk of the preaching and pastoral care is centered on one person, it creates the impression that the person has more authority than the New Testament grants. Once the congregation perceives that the pastor has all the authority, it follows that the pastor also bears all the responsibility for getting everything done. Larry Kreider, Ron May, Steve Prokopchak and Brian Sauder serve together as leaders in DOVE International Ministries. That denomination emphasizes multi-leadership in their churches. Kreider, May, Prokopchak and Sauder worked together to develop training materials on multi-leadership. They write "authority and responsibility must work hand in hand. One cannot claim all authority without accepting all responsibility."[35] This tension between authority and responsibility can be significant. Yet this is exactly what many bivocational pastors face in their churches. The church expects them to provide most of the leadership and manpower in the church as well as accept most of the blame for any faults in the church. Even in those churches which emphasize congregational control more than pastoral leadership, the senior pastor is often still seen as the one most responsible for what goes on in the church. But this is not how the church was led in the New Testament.

In the life of the New Testament church there was an equal sharing of leadership by a group of people. One example of this multiple leadership approach is found in Acts 13:1-3:

> Now there were in the church at Antioch prophets and teachers, Barnabas, Simeon who was called Niger, Lucius of Cyrene, Manaen a member of the court of Herod the tetrarch, and Saul. While they were worshiping the Lord and fasting, the Holy Spirit said, "Set apart for me Barnabas and Saul for the work to which I have called

them." Then after fasting and praying they laid their hands on them and sent them off. (ESV)[36]

This passage demonstrates that five people were serving together as the prophets and teachers of the church in Antioch. Darrell Bock writes in his commentary on Acts that "there appears to be an overlap between the two roles of prophet and teacher for these five; it is not clear if there is any distinction made here in the list as to who did what."[37] The fact that no distinction is made indicates a joint sharing of duties and responsibilities between these five individuals.

It is important to note that the leaders were of different backgrounds, ethnicity, and social standing. Yet they were working together as a team to lead the church in Antioch. Kreider and his co-leaders at DOVE Christian Fellowship International point out that "a plurality of leadership offers an example to the church of working together in love despite differences of opinions and personalities."[38] This plurality also shows that the church does not rise and fall on the leadership of just one person. F. F. Bruce points out in his commentary that "it is perhaps worth noticing that the two men who were to be released for what would nowadays be called missionary service overseas were the two most eminent and gifted leaders in the church."[39] Yet the church would continue on under the leadership of those who remained, a further indication of the shared leadership of all five men.

When pastors find themselves in churches that do not have multiple leaders, developing leaders should be one of the first priorities. Paul's young protégé Timothy found himself in such a situation while he was serving as pastor of the church in Ephesus. Paul wrote a letter to Timothy instructing him in how to lead the church.

Part of those instructions are found in 2 Tim. 2:1-2:

> Timothy, my dear son, be strong through the grace that God gives you in Christ Jesus. You have heard me teach things that have been confirmed by many reliable witnesses. Now teach these truths to other trustworthy people who will be able to pass them on to others. (NLT)[40]

In this passage Paul instructs Timothy to teach other individuals the truth of the gospel. But they were not just any individuals; they were individuals who must be able to share in the teaching ministry of the church. They were to be trustworthy people who would pass the truth of the gospel on to others. Noted theologian Philip Towner points out in his commentary on the letters to Timothy and Titus that "the command is therefore designed primarily to ensure the continuation of the churches' and the mission's ministry in Asia Minor."[41] The emphasis was on Timothy training others who would join him in his teaching, preaching, and leading ministries in the church. Timothy was to raise up others who would help him lead the church. This should be a goal of all pastors, especially those serving in bivocational roles.

Multiple Callings to Ministry Exist in a Healthy Church

The New Testament teaches that there are multiple callings to ministry and that all of them are needed for a healthy church.[42] God calls all Christians to serve Him in a general sense as followers of Christ.[43] God also calls certain people to a deeper level of service to the church.[44] Those people who have been called to a deeper level of service should be working together as a team to make sure all the ministries of the church are accomplished effectively. Calling on their expertise in team ministry,

Roy and Jackie Trueblood point out that "team implies that all members are committed to the same vision or mission. Obviously, and, hopefully, each member will have different ideas about how to accomplish the mission, but there is essential agreement among all on what constitutes the objective."[45] The objective is a healthy church that glorifies God. This can only be achieved as a team of people respond to a call to various forms of leadership.

Different churches use different terms and design various methods to help people discover their different callings in the church. Some churches have very detailed systems to identify and set apart such individuals. Other churches follow less structured methods. Some churches rely on spontaneous utterances from established leaders to help younger people define their unique callings.[46] Some churches place a greater emphasis on having ordained leaders while other churches are comfortable with leaders who are not ordained. Matt Willmington, well known for training young leaders, often meets with people who are trying to decide if they should transition from being volunteers in church to serving in a vocational way. In order to help them discern what type of calling they may be experiencing, he likes to ask these questions:

> What do you mean by 'ministry'?
>
> Is doing ministry just a matter of a paycheck and position?
>
> Do you have to be paid and have a title to minister? Or does God just want you to keep doing it as a volunteer?
>
> What specific role are you interested in playing?[47]

Willmington recognizes that "obviously we are all called as ministers if we are children of God," but what the individuals he counsels are "asking [about is] the vocational calling."[48] Some people will sense a vocational calling; others will not, but all people need to respond to whatever their various types of callings are in order for the church to be healthy.

The terms used to identify people who respond to God's call are also varied. Common terms include: elders, pastors, preachers, messengers of the Word, deacons, bishops, overseers, evangelists and apostles. Kreider and his co-leaders from DOVE Christian Fellowship International point out that "the terminology is not as important as is the clear biblical model of teamwork needed to govern the local church."[49] Alexander Strauch, a noted authority on the subject of biblical leadership, essentially says the same thing when he writes, "whatever terminology you choose to describe local church leaders will have advantages and disadvantages. In the end, every local church is responsible to teach its people the meaning of the terms it uses to describe its spiritual leaders, whether it be elders, overseers, ministers, preachers, or pastors."[50] Whatever the methods of identifying the individuals who are called to deeper levels of service and whatever titles are given to them is less important than the fact that there should be a plurality of individuals who are working together as teams to lead churches.

A key passage that demonstrates different callings in ministry is 1 Tim. 5:17. "Elders who do their work well should be respected and paid well, especially those who work hard at both preaching and teaching. (NLT)"[51] This passage clearly draws a line between the elders who work hard at preaching and teaching and those whose work does not include preaching and teaching. Philip Towner writes that the word *elders* is used to "refer to a recognized group of leaders in the church. The whole wording of the verse may imply different categories within this group."[52] The elders were all leaders and all of them had to be able to teach.[53] Though all elders had to be able to teach, that was not the primary role of all the elders. This verse indicates that some elders had the added responsibilities of being the primary preachers and teachers of the church. Because of the additional time those teaching elders devoted to study, they needed some additional financial support from the congregation. Raymond Collins wrote in his commentary on the letters to Timothy and Titus that "the community has a responsibility to provide for the elders who have a particular function in the community."[54] This support included both respect and financial assistance. This does not imply that teaching elders had to be fully-funded, only that they received some financial support from the church so they could devote additional time to the study and preaching of the Word.

All elders labor for the church in one way or another. Teaching elders spend a larger part of their time laboring in study. Raymond Collins explains that "labor (*kopiao*) describes the ministry of those engaged in the ministry of prophecy and teaching. The use of this verb suggests that the ministry of prophecy and teaching demands effort. It is time-consuming and fatiguing."[55] This passage indicates that while all elders share leadership, there are different kinds of leadership. For the church to be healthy, a plurality of leaders with different ministry callings is needed.

The Local Church Is the Primary Training Experience for Ministry

Modern church attendees in North America have placed so great an emphasis on formal theological training that they have missed the role the church was designed to fill in training people for ministry. In the New Testament, the local church was the primary training experience for ministry. In order to build effective pastoral leadership teams, the church must once again become the preeminent place for ministry training. That is not to say that formal theological training has no value and should not be pursued. It simply means that when such training occurs in isolation from the local church, it has significantly less value than church-based training.

Previously 2 Tim. 2:1-2 was examined in light of the need for multiple leaders. But it also speaks directly to churches serving as the primary training experiences for ministry. In that passage Paul writes:

> Timothy, my dear son, be strong through the grace that God gives you in Christ Jesus. You have heard me teach things that have been confirmed by many reliable witnesses. Now teach these truths to other trustworthy people who will be able to pass them on to others. (NLT)[56]

This passage specifically instructs Timothy to educate leaders so they can train others. This is not just preaching to the congregation; this is training new leaders who will teach the congregation. It is important to note that this training occurred in the context of the local church. Kreider and his co-leaders correctly observed, "the unlimited potential of this kind of in-house training is obvious."[57]

In the confines of current thinking about leadership training in churches, when people express a call to vocational ministry, they are frequently encouraged to go away to seminaries to learn how to fulfill their calling. When they graduate, churches hire them to serve as pastoral leaders. This is very different than how people were trained in the New Testament. Kreider and his co-leaders showed their passion about this subject when they observed that "the early church did not recruit elders from a distant seminary. Seminary experience was not a prerequisite to leadership in the New Testament church, although some leaders, like Paul, were trained theologians, having studied the law under the strict religious sect of the Pharisees."[58] But most of the leaders of the New Testament church were trained on the job as they served alongside other leaders.[59] The local church was the primary training experience for ministry.

Due to the prevalence in the modern church of formal seminary education, few models are available for training ministry leaders in a local church setting. Sensing the growing disconnect between local churches and formal seminary education, the Lilly Endowment funded a study of the future of theological education in 1984. In response to the findings in that study, researcher Susan Willhauck discovered in 2000 that Wesley Theological Seminary "committed to move from being a church-related seminary to a church-centered seminary" in an effort to "recruit 200 congregations and 2000 individuals into a formal partnership program" with the seminary.[60] Much of the energy for this shift came from the school's new president, David McAllister-Wilson, and his stated goal was to "connect Wesley with congregations in a more significant way."[61] Though still a formal program operated by a seminary, it is an attempt to reengage the local church in participating in the education of their pastors. It is hoped that by reengaging the local church in the training of pastors that Wesley can close the gap between the kind of training typically offered in seminaries and the kind of leaders churches actually need.

St. Gabriel's Catholic Parish in New Orleans has taken ministry training one additional step. Barbara Fleischer did an extensive case study of St. Gabriel's. She noted that they believe that "religious education occurs in the context of community, which in turn focuses outward to ever-widening social and ecological contexts of ministerial action."[62] Because of this strong conviction of ministry training in the context of community, St. Gabriel's Parish wanted their ministry students to remain on site in the religious community of the local church. They recruited ten pastoral team members who agreed to give eight to ten hours a week in ministry leadership for five years. These pastoral team members were enrolled in the Loyola Institute for Ministry Extension program and one-half of the courses in that program were taught on site. Like the Wesley program, St. Gabriel's effort still had a formal academic element, but also a significant local church component.

The efforts by Wesley Seminary and St. Gabriel's Parish are supported by a strong understanding of Tit. 1:5-9:

> The reason I left you in Crete was to set right what was left undone and, as I directed you, to appoint elders in every town: someone who is blameless, the husband of one wife, having faithful children not accused of wildness or rebellion. For an overseer, as God's manager, must be blameless, not arrogant, not quick tempered, not addicted to wine, not a bully, not greedy for money, but hospitable, loving what is good, sensible, righteous, holy, self-controlled, holding to the faithful message as taught, so that he will be able both to encourage with sound teaching and to refute those who contradict it. (HCSV)[63]

This passage indicates that Paul left Titus on Crete to finish what was left undone, which was the appointment and training of leaders for the churches. Theologian Raymond Collins commented that Paul "portrays Titus as someone who has been charged with the responsibility for the good order of the church on the island of Crete."[64] Notice that Titus was not instructed to accomplish this by gathering the leaders together and sending them off to some formal seminary in a distant place. The indication is that he was to train them in place.

These leaders were not just secondary helpers charged with menial tasks that Titus did not want to do. They were to be overseers of the church with significant responsibilities. Raymond Collins wrote that "the overseer is a teacher in the community of faith. His responsibility is to exhort the members of the community with sound teaching and to correct opponents. If he is to do that, he must hang on to the trustworthy saying [of scripture] in accordance with the norm of the community's teaching."[65] These leaders were given the charge to teach the scriptures to the congregations they led. They were also given the charge to refute those who were teaching false doctrine. Philip Towner emphasizes in his commentary that "the term that describes this activity includes revealing falsehood, correction, and rebuke."[66] It is one thing to be able to give a proper lesson to those who agree with you. It is quite another to rebuke a person who is teaching a false theology. The fact that the overseers were expected to do this speaks to the highly developed level of their training and abilities, all of which was formed in the context of the local church.

Conclusion

The modern North American church has forgotten its history and theology of church leadership. This lack of understanding of the historical biblical context has led to a confusing application of church leadership principles in the present. As the church rediscovers that bivocational ministry is normal, it will help remove some of the negative stigma that is often associated with bivocational ministry. As the church rediscovers that shared pastoral leadership is both biblical and more emotionally healthy for the pastors, it will remove significant pressure from pastors serving in single leadership situations. As the church rediscovers the importance of all its members knowing and fulfilling various types of callings to ministry, key people will emerge who can help provide team leadership to the church. As the church rediscovers its own role in training people for ministry, such ministerial training will be more church-based and therefore more practical and beneficial to the church. With a better understanding of these theological principles, pastors and churches can examine the practical realities of applying these theological principles to their unique situations.

Chapter 3

What are the Current Relevant Trends in North America?

Applying the theological principles of building effective pastoral leadership teams requires having a working knowledge of current cultural trends affecting bivocational pastors and the churches they serve. A failure to understand these trends and methods will lead to frustration and ineffectiveness. Dennis Bickers has written numerous books about bivocational ministry, he laments that too many pastors are "more dreamers than visionaries. They often understand the needs of their churches but have no idea as to how to achieve them."[67] Helping pastors move beyond dreaming to actually seeing the fulfillment of God's vision for their churches is critical. The first step of moving from dream to fulfillment is grasping the reality of the current situation. This chapter will help pastors understand four significant trends impacting the modern church.

Bivocational Ministry Is Becoming More Common

A key cultural trend is that bivocational ministry is becoming more common in North American Protestant churches. Regardless of how pastors and/or church attendees may feel about bivocational ministry, it is a growing practice in North American church life. Patricia Chang is a research professor at Boston College and has studied many denominations and written extensively about clergy issues. Chang has done extensive research on how bivocational ministry is impacting American denominations of all sizes and theological persuasions. In a major study published in the *Pulpit and Pew* journal of Duke University, Chang concludes that "the majority of congregations in the United States are small, with fewer than 100 regular members, and cannot typically afford their own pastor."[68] This results in a growing need for more bivocational pastors every year. Chang is not alone in her conclusions. Linda Lawson studied America's largest Protestant denomination, the Southern Baptist Convention, and predicted in 1999 that "if present trends continue, bivocational Southern Baptist pastors will outnumber full-time pastors [fully-funded] within 10 years."[69] Though it is difficult to track the exact number of bivocational pastors within that denomination, the Southern Baptist Bivocational Ministers Association (SBBMA) asserts on their website that "there are almost 30,000 churches that reported an average Sunday School attendance of fewer than 125 in 2006. Most of these are bivocational."[70] Lifeway Research reports that same year that the denomination had a total of 44,366 churches.[71] If what the SBBMA asserts is accurate, then the prediction from ten years ago was correct and now the number of bivocational pastors within the SBC exceeds the number of fully-funded pastors. This information is difficult to verify conclusively, but it clearly speaks to the trend toward bivocational ministry that is growing within the Southern Baptist Convention.

The Southern Baptist Convention is not the only denomination experiencing significant growth in the number of bivocational pastors. Patricia Chang's findings demonstrate that "the current religious landscape is skewed towards a very large number of small congregations and a small number of large congregations."[72] Most of those small congregations are unable to fully-fund their pastors, resulting in those churches seeking bivocational pastors to guide them.

By understanding how common their situation is, bivocational pastors do not need to have negative feelings about their status. Bivocational ministry is a growing reality of ministry in North American Protestant church life. Dennis Bickers reminds bivocational pastors that he works with to "never let the misconceptions others may have about your ministry cause you to question your call and your value to the work of the kingdom of God."[73] Bivocational pastors are not second-class ministers. They are an important and growing segment of American church life.

Pastors Experience Burn-Out If They Do Not Delegate

A second trend that is important to understand is the increasing number of pastors experiencing burn-out. The number of pastors who enter this downward emotional spiral has been growing in recent years. Bob Wells is a colleague of Patricia Chang and has done extensive research on the health of American clergy. In a 2002 article in *Pulpit and Pew,* Wells concluded that "doctrinal and theological differences aside, North American churches have in common not only the Cross and a love of Christ, but also a pastorate whose health is fast becoming cause for concern."[74] Pastors are not as healthy as they should be. This lack of health contributes to the higher burn-out rates currently being experienced by pastors.

Many factors contribute to this lack of health. Some are physiological; some are psychological. One of the factors that lead to burn-out is loneliness. When pastors do not feel they have anyone with whom to share their burdens, they feel isolated and alone. Even with all his successful bivocational ministry experience, Dennis Bickers still laments that, "Sometimes ministry is a very lonely place."[75] Loneliness can lead to depression. When pastors feel depressed, they are more vulnerable to emotional fatigue, to the practice of unhealthy habits, and to increased levels of anxiety. These factors greatly decrease pastors' effectiveness in ministry. Fred Lehr, a consultant for the Evangelical Lutheran Church and founder of Renewal Ministries, worked with burned out pastors for many years at the Church Renewal Center in Allentown, Pennsylvania. His experience indicates that "depressed clergy are not effective clergy."[76] Pastors who feel ineffective in their ministries have increased negative emotions, which in turn increase the likelihood of burn-out. Therefore, systems must be put in place to help pastors overcome feelings of depression so they can be healthier individuals and more effective in their ministries. When such systems are not in place, pastors become trapped in a downward spiral that feeds upon itself until they become emotionally paralyzed in ministry and in their personal lives.

Unfortunately, loneliness and depression are just part of the problem. The general brokenness of modern society brings additional challenges to pastors who are seeking to bring healing to their communities. In that same *Pulpit and Pew* article, Bob Wells reported that "faced with overwhelming need and filled with a genuine desire to help, many pastors, consciously or not, set themselves up for problems, thanks in part to a misguided notion of ministry."[77] H. B. London, of Focus on the Family, writes, "Today's pastors face crises unknown to any other occupational groups. Contemporary parish ministry, without anyone intending to make it so, has become an emotional and spiritual H-bomb, ready to explode any second."[78] Loneliness, depression, a compulsion to fix society, and the internal politics of local churches combine together to make pastoral ministry a difficult calling to fulfill. Yet God has called people to this important task and the call must be answered.

Pastors working outside jobs, in addition to serving churches, are even more likely than fully-funded pastors to experience burn-out and leave the field of service. While all pastors face the same challenges, based on his years of experience, Dennis Bickers concludes that "bivocational pastors usually face those challenges with less formal education, training, and resources, but that does not mean they are doomed to be defeated."[79] As bivocational pastors are taught how to build pastoral leadership teams, they will be less prone to feelings of loneliness. As bivocational pastors learn to share the burdens of ministry with an entire team, they will no longer feel as overwhelmed. Building pastoral leadership teams can help pastors avoid feeling burned out.

Building pastoral leadership teams requires a willingness to delegate some duties to others. Delegation, the lifeline many ministers must grasp to avoid burn-out, will be a challenge for some bivocational pastors to practice. Dennis Bickers has learned over the years that "most bivocational ministers are type A personalities who are hardworking, aggressive, and competitive. Laziness is seldom a problem for these people."[80] The very fact that bivocational pastors are willing to work two jobs to follow the call of God demonstrates their work ethic. They are the kind of people who get the job done, even if it means they must do it themselves. But this type A personality can be as much a curse as a blessing if not channeled in healthy ways.

Bivocational pastors must learn to resist the temptation to work themselves to exhaustion. Exhaustion quickly leads to burnout. Dennis Bickers emphasizes that "the bivocational pastor has to come to terms with the fact that he may never pastor the biggest church in the community, or else he is going to become miserable and frustrated."[81] Leading the biggest church or having the most programs or the nicest church building should not be the goal. The goal should be to bring glory to God in all things. One way God is glorified is when pastors and churches follow the leadership principles described in the New Testament. When those leadership principles are followed and bringing glory to God becomes the goal, then working oneself to exhaustion is no longer necessary.

Phil Newton, who has served in pastoral ministry for thirty years and has been an adjunct professor at several schools, emphasizes the necessity and value of delegating responsibilities in his book, *Elders in Congregational Life: Rediscovering the Biblical Model for Church Leadership*. He reminds pastors that delegation is not just about passing off a list of tasks to others. Delegation means giving up control and sharing leadership with others. While some pastors may fear this, delegation actually helps pastors be more effective because it helps them see the blind spots in ministry which they have missed on their own. Newton writes, "Non-staff elders see some things that those involved in full-time [fully-funded] ministry cannot. Those of us in vocational ministry find this difficult to admit. The constant saturation of experience within the walls of ministry, however, may skew a pastor's thinking on congregational expectations and needs."[82] Raising up effective pastoral leadership teams makes the entire church more effective than what any individual leader, no matter how gifted, can do on his or her own.

Delegating menial tasks may be easier to do, but for delegation to really help, pastors must also be willing to delegate some of the preaching and pastoral care duties. Because these are two of the most time-consuming and emotionally-draining aspects of ministry, a failure to delegate a portion of these duties will result in pastors still not having time to rest. Alexander Strauch has written a number of excellent books to help pastors train deacons and elders in their churches to share the load of ministry. Strauch notes that "it is a highly significant but often overlooked fact that our Lord did not appoint one man to lead His church. He personally appointed and trained twelve men."[83] These were not twelve men who helped with menial tasks but men Jesus sent out to preach, teach, and address the needs of people. Pastors need to follow the example of Jesus and recruit help in their preaching and pastoral care efforts. As pastors learn to give away part of their ministry to others, they will have less stress. Less stress will help them avoid burn-out and stay in their ministry positions longer.

Helping pastors discover the joy of longevity in ministry is a key to helping them live happier and healthier lives. Lengthening the longevity of pastoral leadership is also vital to long-term church health. The importance of longevity in pastoral ministry became evident through research done by George Barna. Barna's research indicated the following:

- Because viable churches are based on relationship and because a strong community takes time to build, the possibility of a pastor creating a strong relational network within the congregation is minimized by a short tenure.

- Many pastors experience their most productive years in ministry between their third and fifteenth years of service. Leaving after four years or so removes the prospect of exploiting the prime years of influence.

- When churches experience a revolving door pastorate, they are less likely to be trusting, communal and outward oriented. A major influence of short pastoral tenures causes the congregation to assume a protective, inward-looking perspective.[84]

Longevity in ministry simply makes pastors and churches healthier. Pastors are healthier because they are able to build the needed relational networks for their own emotional health. Churches are healthier because they learn to trust their pastors, and that trust translates into a willingness to try new ideas and reach out to more people.

When pastors are unhealthy, they tend to change churches more frequently in an attempt to relieve stress and/or rediscover joy in ministry. But if the pastors' work habits are the real problem, then they take those problems with them to the next church and experience those same difficulties all over again. When churches are not healthy they become even more of a burden on the pastors who serve them, further exasperating pastors. The cycle of unhealthy pastors serving unhealthy churches breeds on itself in a never ending pattern. What is needed to break these unhealthy patterns is for pastors to be willing to stay longer at each church they serve. As the pastors build relationships with others in the church, those relationships serve as bulwarks against loneliness, depression, and a dangerous "I can do it all myself" attitude. As the pastors become healthier, the churches become healthier. When churches become healthier, then pastors do not feel as overwhelmed. A pattern of health for both pastors and churches emerges when pastoral longevity is increased.

Barna goes on to say that "the data indicates that the smaller the church body the more likely the pastor is to spend only a few years in that pulpit."[85] This means that smaller churches, which are more likely to be led by bivocational pastors, are especially prone to short term pastorates and therefore likely to be less healthy. If pastors are already dealing with loneliness, depression, lack of self-esteem, and an overwhelming work load, they do not need unhealthy churches to deal with as well. However, much of this can be avoided if pastors will delegate some of the responsibilities to others. Delegation leads to healthier pastors. Healthier pastors do not burn-out but stay at their churches longer. The longer pastors stay in their churches, the healthier the churches become. The healthier the churches become, the more God is glorified and the more joy pastors have as they serve.

Pastoral burn-out is a real issue in modern church life, but it is an issue that can be addressed. While there are many ways to address this problem, this book focuses on helping pastors learn to train up multiple leaders so they can delegate some of their preaching and pastoral care duties to them.

Laymen Can and Will Help if Trained Effectively

A third key trend impacting the church is the willingness of the laity to work in greater partnership with the clergy. Common thought among many ministry leaders is that the laity does not want to be involved in church work. H. B. London, of Focus on the Family, writes, "Pastors serve in a me-centered world where church members and attenders are becoming more and more apathetic."[86] While London's assessment may be true, one must ask if pastors are training their congregations to be part of the solution or part of the problem. Fred Lehr works with pastors who have become burned out. He writes in his book, *Clergy Burnout: Recovering from the Seventy Hour Work Week and Other Self Defeating Practices* that "the volume of responsibilities dumped on the clergy is inordinate, and because we clergy are so codependent, we accept that burden, rescue the laity from their responsibilities, and suffer the consequences."[87] Pastors must begin to learn how to help the laity accept more responsibility. Pastors must learn to let go of their own need to be in control. Pastors need to address their desires to personally solve all the problems in the church. Dennis Bickers has learned that "many lay people want to be more involved in the church's ministry in the community and are just waiting to be asked."[88] Pastors may be surprised just how much lay people are willing to do if only they are asked.

Simply making announcements before worship services that pastors need help will probably not produce the level of commitment needed to provide significant assistance to pastors. Dennis Bickers correctly observes that "a bivocational minister should not expect to find lay leaders who are capable of serving on leadership teams without investing time and energy in training them."[89] Pastors must make time to develop leaders. Pastors must set priorities in their own schedules so they can train others to help them. Pastors must then be willing to release significant responsibilities to the individuals they train.

Pastors should make sure their sermons include teaching on spiritual gifts and the importance of using those gifts for God. Pastors must find ways to highlight practical examples of what lay people can do to help lead the church. Dennis Bickers frequently reminds pastors that "the first step is to help the lay people understand how important it is for them to be involved in ministry."[90] Once lay people begin to understand that they are needed and gifted for ministry, they will be more willing to accept responsibility for ministry leadership.

While many people would agree that lay people can effectively lead in certain areas of ministry, they may not feel as confident that lay people can preach and accomplish pastoral care duties effectively. However, with the right encouragement and training, lay people in the church can be taught how to deliver an effective sermon and do basic pastoral care. Not only can they be taught this, but many people are willing to do these things if they are trained properly.

Pastors must begin to understand how important it is for them to be raising up individuals who can preach and do pastoral care. Kreider and his co-leaders emphasize this in every church within their denomination. They make it clear that "an elder [pastor] must learn to train and release others. He must be proactive in giving away his responsibilities to others whom he is raising up in ministry."[91] Pastors should not wait for people to step forward and volunteer. They should be constantly looking for parishioners with leadership potential. Pastors should have an ongoing and intentional plan for discovering, enlisting, training, and releasing lay people for the ministry of preaching and pastoral care.

Building effective pastoral leadership teams will not be an easy task. Differences in personalities, communication styles, and life experiences will be obstacles to be overcome for effective teams to emerge. Drawing on his years of research, George Barna concludes that "a team mentality does not spontaneously arise with the church. A leader must instill the vision for team play among the players and create an environment in which those players work together toward a common end. The objective is to glorify God through acts of personal spiritual growth and community service."[92] Though the challenges to building such team environments in the church are significant, the end result is worth it.

Formal Theological Education Is Helpful But Not Necessary

The final trend for pastors of small churches to recognize is that while a formal theological education is helpful, it is not necessary for a person to accomplish effective ministry. Some church and/or denominational leaders may feel that teaching lay people to preach and giving them significant pastoral duties will weaken the church. One regional coordinator for a major North American denomination expressed his concerns regarding lay leadership in an article in *Word and World*:

> In contrast, some synods in the ELCA have tried to assist struggling congregations with lay preachers, only to watch congregational giving and benevolence shrink. There are anecdotal reports of loss of mission awareness and even moves to leave the denomination as a result of the work of lay preachers. The ELCA has a very finely crafted candidacy process for professional leaders. In contrast, lay leadership currently has no formal guidelines, and expectations vary from synod to synod. This must be remedied. In a nation of highly educated members who are part of a culture of very sophisticated communication and unlimited information, we cannot afford to provide anything less than the best possible gospel preaching. Quality may not be guaranteed by using trained clergy, but it will certainly not be served by employing inadequately prepared and unaccountable lay preachers.[93]

Clearly this particular denominational leader does not think highly of lay preachers. His inference to a highly-educated culture accustomed to sophisticated communication implies that he does not believe lay preachers are capable of communicating effectively to such educated people. He thinks very highly of the finely crafted system his denomination has created to develop a professional clergy. But one must ask why that denomination is still experiencing a clergy shortage if the system of developing professional clergy is so well constructed.

To be fair to this particular denominational leader, this same type of negative attitude is frequently found in articles about lay preaching. The underlying idea of many denominational leaders is that lay people cannot preach as well as seminary trained professional clergy. If this is indeed an accurate assessment, one must ask what the key difference is between professional clergy and lay people. The most obvious answer is training. If lay people are given adequate training, then there would be no reason to expect inadequate preaching and pastoral care from them.

While there may be some voices of concern regarding the quality of lay preachers, a rising chorus of voices is also calling for increased training for lay ministers so they can be as effective as possible. DOVE Christian Fellowship International is a family of churches throughout the world that are each led by a combination of professional and lay elders. The leaders of that movement remind their constituents to "make no mistake: studying for church leadership is very helpful for eldership and is not to be discouraged."[94] DOVE leaders have developed resources and written a book on how to develop quality leaders in the churches affiliated with their group. They believe strongly in leadership training; they just do not think it is necessary for every person to go to seminary in order to get that training.

Steve Nerger makes his position about the relationship between formal education and lay leaders clear in his book, *Bivocational Church Planters: Uniquely Wired for Kingdom Growth*. He writes, "Please, do not misunderstand. God has a unique calling for pastors. We are not trying to diminish that. However, this calling is not just for seminary-trained men. That is a North American mistake created by the arrogance of humankind with the prestige of a human-made education."[95] Like the leaders of DOVE, Nerger recognizes the role of formal theological education in training ministry leaders; he just believes that people have gotten so focused on formal education that they may have missed the bigger implications of God's calling on a person's life to serve in ministry. When God calls people to serve Him, God will help those people answer that calling regardless of the level of their formal theological education.

Diane Melbye, an attorney in North Dakota who serves on the board of trustees at Luther Seminary, offers this reminder in a 2004 article in *Word and World*: "Scripture affirms that none of the original disciples had completed seminary training or been ordained prior to being sent forth to preach the gospel!"[96] What a powerful reminder that the church was built by lay people willing to answer the call to be on a team of preachers that changed the world.

This book will help bivocational pastors train selected individuals to join them in preaching and pastoral care. The training process put forth in this book does not seek to diminish the value of a formal theological education, but instead seeks to recognize the reality that such an education is not necessary for people to be effective in preaching and pastoral care.

Conclusion

As bivocational pastors begin the process of raising up pastoral leadership teams, they will need to understand four current cultural trends facing the North American church. First, they will need to grasp the reality that their role as bivocational pastors is becoming more common. Bivocational ministry is quickly becoming the norm instead of the exception. Second, bivocational pastors will need to realize that they are more prone to burn-out than fully-funded pastors. Bivocational pastors will need to understand that they can avoid this dilemma if they begin building pastoral leadership teams to assist them in ministry. This may require bivocational pastors to rethink their responsibilities and expectations for themselves. But such introspection will be profitable for both the pastors and the churches they serve. Third, bivocational pastors will have to help laypeople understand they are gifted and able to help lead the church. This will not happen automatically. While it will take an investment of time and energy, it will also reap long term benefits for both the pastors and the churches. Finally, bivocational pastors will need to understand the value of adequate training for the lay people they seek to raise up to help them in ministry. While such training might be found through formal theological education, it will frequently be found through experience and self study on the field of service. When pastors come to understand these four trends, they will be ready to embark on the journey of discovering, enlisting, training, and releasing their pastoral leadership teams for effective ministry.

Chapter 4

Steps for Gathering and Training the Team

This chapter will outline the six steps which pastors can follow in order to gather and prepare people to be part of a team approach to preaching and pastoral care. The steps are briefly outlined below.

The first step will be for pastors to recruit lay people who are interested in being part of a team approach to ministry. This may initially be done via announcements from the pulpit or a mailing to all the members of the congregation which explains the general concept of this approach to ministry and the benefits participants can expect to gain. But announcements or mailings alone will not be adequate. Such announcements or mailings will need to be followed by personal contacts to specific individuals whom the pastors feel are most likely to participate, based on their experience with their congregations. A failure to engage in personalized follow up will likely result in few, if any, volunteers for such an endeavor. Though this personalized follow up may take considerable time in the beginning, the end result will be worth the initial investment of time and energy.

The second step is for pastors to begin to meet with interested lay people in a series of six extended training sessions. Each of the six sessions will have three fifty-five minute segments. The first segment will address the preaching aspect of the training. The second segment will address the pastoral care aspect of the training. The third segment will include actual preaching experiences and/or role plays by the lay people. These experiences will be evaluated by both the participants and the pastors. Each session will last a total of three hours, for a total of eighteen hours of classroom training.

The third step will begin after the third classroom session has been completed by the lay people. That step will involve the pastors taking the lay people on a series of three pastoral visits. On the first visit, the pastors will model an effective visit while the lay people observe. On the second visit, the pastors will assign the lay people some portion of the visit to lead. On the third visit, the pastors will allow the lay people to lead the entire visit while the pastors are silent partners in the visit. After each visit the pastors will discuss the experience with the lay people and suggest what improvements, if any, need to be made.

The fourth step will take place after the final classroom session. After the lay people have completed all the required classroom sessions, the pastors will schedule a time for the lay people to preach in their own churches. The pastors will also cooperate with other pastors in nearby churches or with denominational leaders to help the lay people schedule times to preach in nearby churches. The pastors, along with other individuals whom they will select from the congregation, will be asked to evaluate the sermons using an assessment tool that has been developed specifically for this training process. The assessment tool will be filled out after the worship service and given to the pastors. The pastors will help the lay people interpret the assessment tool and continue to work with the lay people on improving their preaching skills based on weaknesses and strengths revealed in the assessment tool. The assessment tool may be used as long as the pastor and lay people think it is needed so that continual feedback and improvements can be made to the preaching skills of the lay people.

The fifth step will be for the pastors and the lay people to work together to develop a written process to address how they will continue to serve as a team in preaching and pastoral care after the initial six session training project is completed. This will include suggestions for further training in both preaching and pastoral care from such sources as are available to the pastors and lay people.

The sixth step will be to recognize all the lay people who complete the entire training project. The pastors are encouraged to recognize the lay people during a Sunday morning service and award them a certificate of completion. Pastors can create their own certificate, or they can purchase a certificate from an educational supply store. Recognizing the achievements of the lay people not only gives them a great sense of satisfaction, but it also helps the churches understand the new level of leadership the lay people will be assuming.

Chapter 5

Introduction to Preaching and Pastoral Care

Two of the most fulfilling ministries pastors participate in are preaching and pastoral care. The preaching of the Word of God changes lives and countless pastors testify to how God uses their preaching to heal broken hearts, restore marriages, comfort the grieving and challenge the saints to greater service to the Lord. Pastoral care has many facets, but for the purposes of this book, pastoral care will be defined as making a personal visit to a person that is in need of spiritual comfort or encouragement. It is not to be confused with pastoral counseling, which may require a much greater degree of training than this six session process can offer. While these two ministries are the most fulfilling, they are also often the most time consuming. Both sermon preparation and pastoral care can consume the greater part of the pastors' day. While this may be fine for fully-funded pastors, when pastors have to work an additional job to support their families, these are often the two ministry areas that suffer most. Therefore if lay people really want to help their pastors, they need to be willing to share the burden of these two ministry areas with their pastor. This chapter will introduce lay people to what it takes to prepare sermons and perform basic pastoral care.

Session One Teaching Plan

Welcome and Greeting Time (25 minutes)

- Call on one of the lay people to open the session in prayer. It is important from the very beginning of the training that the lay people be encouraged to take leadership. If the pastors say all the prayers and lead all the discussions, it sets a poor example on the value of lay leadership.

- The pastor should share about why he feels called to ministry. This should be kept to five minutes or less so as not to become a mini-sermon.

- The pastor should then ask each person to share about their own interest in receiving ministry training and what one benefit is they hope to gain from these sessions.

- Distribute the syllabus (appendix B) and explain the purpose of the training and how it will proceed.

Learning to Preach Segment (40 minutes)

- Post three large sheets of paper around the room. Each of the sheets will have one of these three questions written at the top; Why do we preach? What do we preach? How do we preach? Ask each person to write a response on each the sheets.

- "Why Should We Preach? and "What Should We Preach?" Guide a 20 minute discussion on the importance of preaching and the need to make preaching based on scripture, not on personal opinions. Teach through 1 Corinthians 1:18 (KJV) "For the preaching of the cross is to them that perish foolishness; but unto us which are saved it is the power of God." Emphasize that people preach in order to persuade, motivate, and convince. Contrast that with teaching, which primarily educates, informs, or organizes theology. Point out that often preaching includes some teaching and teaching may include some preaching, but if preachers remember why they preach, they will be more focused in their sermons. Refer to Isaiah 55:11 (KJV) "So shall my word be that goes forth out of my mouth: it shall not return unto me void, but it shall accomplish that which I please, and it shall prosper in the thing whereto I sent it." Emphasize the importance of preaching the Word of God instead of human opinions because the Word has supernatural power but human opinion has very little power. Incorporate the students' responses from the first two large sheets into the discussion.

- After the discussion, gauge how well the students grasped the concepts by asking "What is the difference between preaching and teaching?" Allow five minutes for the class to discuss this. Then ask the group to discuss why sermons need to focus on scripture instead of human opinion.

- How Should We Preach? The pastor should share for ten minutes about the different types of sermons that he has utilized over the years. Feel free to invite a guest pastor to share in this portion of the training to provide a broader view of ideas.

- Refer to the third large sheet and see how many of the students had the same types of sermons listed as what the pastor suggested from his own experience.

- Use the "Types of Sermons" handout to present the different types of sermons that can be used. Briefly explain each type. Emphasize that though all types of sermons should be utilized at appropriate times, expository preaching will produce the most biblically literate believers over the long term.

- Distribute the "Importance of Expository Sermons" outline. Briefly explain why expository preaching is so important. Suggest that the students consider purchasing William Evan's book, *How to Prepare Sermons*.

- Ask if there are any questions and discuss whatever they may be.

Take a ten-minute break.

Learning to Make Visits Segment (50 minutes)

- The pastor should introduce the session by sharing a personal testimony of a meaningful pastoral visit that helped his own spiritual development.

- Then ask each person to recall a time when a pastor visited them at a crucial point in their lives. Ask them how that visit made them feel. Explain that visiting is often called pastoral care. But a visit is only pastoral care if the purpose of the visit includes a spiritual aspect and not just fellowship. Discuss the difference between a friendly visit and a pastoral care visit. In a friendly visit, the discussion may be about the family, or the weather, or who won the ball game. A pastoral care visit may also discuss those things, but will include scripture reading and prayer.

- Ask the group to think of as many reasons as they can that a person in the church might need a pastoral care visit. Write their responses on a white board. If the students miss any key reasons that a person might need a pastoral care visit, the pastor should suggest them at the end of the discussion.

- Lead a discussion on how a person can make a good pastoral care visit. Use the "Effective and Healthy Pastoral Visit" handout. During this discussion, remind the students that a pastoral care visit is different than pastoral counseling. A visit is intended to express care and concern, not necessarily solve a problem or give advice. Solving problems and giving advice are better suited for pastoral counseling. This training is not designed to develop pastoral counselors. This training is designed to help the students be effective in making pastoral care visits. Emphasize this to the students and help them understand that there could be legal liabilities for providing counseling to others if one is not trained to do so.

- Close this portion of the session by asking the group what makes them the most nervous about making pastoral visits. Have the group spend time in prayer for those expressed concerns.

Take a ten-minute break.

Practical Application Segment (45 minutes)

NOTE: These role plays are designed to reinforce what was taught in the first two segments. The point of the role plays each week is to help those students whose learning styles may not be geared toward auditory learning. It also allows the pastor to use some humor as a way to make some key points about the need for training lay people in these skills.

- "Pastor Is Going Out of Town" role play - Ask two students to read aloud a pre-written role play about the pastor going out of town and there being no substitute pastor available to preach. Assure the students that acting ability is not needed and that no prior practice is required.

- After the two students have finished reading the role play, ask if a similar scenario has ever happened in real life and discuss the probable likelihood of it happening in a small church.

- "The Worst Visit Ever" role play - Ask two students to read aloud a role play about a pastoral visit in which the person who makes the visit does everything wrong. The pastor should make sure a person is not selected who may be known for being guilty of the mistakes suggested in the role play. It may be necessary for the pastor to play the role of the "bad visitor" in order to keep from type casting a student.

- After the role play ends, ask the group to discuss all the things wrong with the visit. It is hoped that they will recall what was taught in the previous segment about elements of a good visit.

- Give an assignment for the next session by asking the lay people to bring their favorite Bible study books with them to the next session.

Session Evaluation

- Pass out the evaluation form for this session and ask the group to take a few minutes to fill it in and return it to the pastor. Explain to the students that an evaluation form will be turned in each week at the conclusion of the class. The responses on the form will help the pastor know what the students grasped and what needs to be reinforced in a future session.

- Ask one of the students to close the session with prayer.

Types of Sermons – Leader's Key

1. Expository Sermons - this is when a pastor preaches through an entire book of the Bible one verse at a time. He may teach several verses in a particular week, but he will deal with each verse one at a time. The following week he will go on to the next section. It may take him months to get through a book of the Bible. Each sermon is really part of a long series of sermons.

2. Textual Sermons - this is when a pastor preaches about a particular verse, or set of verses. He may give the same type of explanation as you might hear in an expository sermon, but the next week he does not go to the next section. He might go to an entirely different part of the Bible. Each sermon is a "stand alone" sermon.

3. Biographical Sermons - this is when a pastor preaches about a particular Bible character. The pastor explains the successes and failures of that person and what we can learn from his or her life.

4. Historical Incident Sermons - this is similar to a biographical sermon except that this type of sermon focuses on a particular incident in the Bible instead of a person in the Bible.

5. Topical Sermons - this is when a pastor uses lots of different scriptures from lots of different parts of the Bible to give a more complete teaching about a particular topic.

6. Personal Testimony - this is when a pastor primarily tells the story of his life or some portion of his life. The pastor uses scriptures to illustrate various moments in life when he learned some specific spiritual truth.

Each type of sermon has its own strengths and weaknesses. Each can be used effectively and each can be abused. The key is to find a scripture and build a sermon around it instead of starting with a human opinion and then trying to prove your opinion with scripture.

Types of Sermons – Student Worksheet

1. _____ Sermons - this is when a pastor preaches through an entire _____ of the Bible one _____ at a time. He may teach several verses in a particular week, but he will deal with each verse one at a time. The following week he will go on to the _____ section. It may take him months to get through a book of the Bible. Each sermon is really part of a long _____ of sermons.

2. _____ Sermons - this is when a pastor preaches about a particular _____, or set of verses. He may give the same type of explanation as you might hear in an expository sermon, but the next week he does not go to the _____ section. He might go to an entirely _____ part of the Bible. Each sermon is a "_____" sermon.

3. _____ Sermons - this is when a pastor preaches about a particular Bible _____. The pastor explains the successes and failures of that _____ and what we can _____ from his or her life.

4. _____ Incident Sermons - this is similar to a biographical sermon except that this type of sermon focuses on a particular _____ in the Bible instead of a person in the Bible.

5. _____ Sermons - this is when a pastor uses lots of _____ scriptures from lots of different _____ of the Bible to give a more _____ teaching about a particular topic.

6. _____ Testimony - this is when a pastor primarily tells the _____ of his life or some portion of his life. The pastor uses scriptures to _____ various moments in life when he learned some specific spiritual truth.

Each type of sermon has its own strengths and weaknesses. Each can be used effectively and each can be abused. The key is to find a scripture and build a sermon around it instead of starting with a human opinion and then trying to prove your opinion with scripture.

IMPORTANCE OF EXPOSITORY SERMONS – LEADER'S GUIDE

Though there are many different types of sermons and each should be used in appropriate ways, the expository sermon is often considered the most important in producing a biblically literate church. Evan Williams' classic book, *How to Prepare Sermons* gives a number of excellent ideas regarding expository sermons. They are summarized below:

An expository sermon is a type of sermon that deals more fully with the explanation of the scripture itself than any other type of sermon.

Advantages of expository sermons:

- It produces biblical preachers and hearers.

- It conforms to the biblical ideal of preaching.

- It is wider in scope than any other type of sermon.

The possible disadvantages of expository sermons:

- It can become monotonous for the congregation.

- The preacher can become lazy if he doesn't actually dig into the meaning.

- The text may be too long. Therefore, keep the sections short enough to deal with in one sermon.

- Such sermons can become too confining because they might ignore current events. To avoid this, utilize other types of sermons from time to time even if one prefers the expository sermon most of the time.

Suggestions for successful expository sermons:

- Use a portion of scripture that contains one leading thought or theme.

- Consider preaching through an Old Testament book and then a New Testament book as a way to balance law and grace.

- A thorough study of the entire text is absolutely critical for the success of an expository sermon.

- The preacher must avoid being merely theoretical; he must be practical as well.

Above outline adapted from Evans, William, How to Prepare Sermons (Chicago: Moody Bible Institute, 1964), pages 92-97.

IMPORTANCE OF EXPOSITORY SERMONS - STUDENT'S WORKSHEET

Though there are many different types of sermons and each should be used in appropriate ways, the _____ sermon is often considered the most important in producing a biblically _____ church. Evan Williams' classic book, *How to Prepare Sermons* gives a number of excellent ideas regarding expository sermons. They are summarized below:

An expository sermon is a type of sermon that deals more fully with the explanation of the _____ itself than any other type of sermon.

Advantages of expository sermons:

- It produces biblical _____ and hearers.

- It conforms to the biblical _____ of preaching.

- It is wider in _____ than any other type of sermon.

The possible disadvantages of expository sermons:

- It can become _____ for the congregation.

- The preacher can become _____ if he doesn't actually dig into the meaning.

- The text may be too _____. Therefore, keep the sections short enough to deal with in one sermon.

- Such sermons can become too confining because they might ignore _____. To avoid this, utilize other types of sermons from time to time even if one prefers the expository sermon most of the time.

Suggestions for expository sermons:

- Use a portion of scripture that contains one leading _____ or theme.

- Consider preaching through an Old Testament book and then a New Testament book as a way to balance _____ and _____.

- A thorough study of the _____ text is an absolutely critical for the success of an expository sermon.

- The preacher must avoid being merely theoretical; he must be _____ as well.

Above outline adapted from: Evans, William, How to Prepare Sermons (Chicago: Moody Bible Institute, 1964), pages 92-97.

Effective and Healthy Pastoral Visits - Leader's Key

Effective and healthy pastoral visits include:

- Focus on the <u>person</u> being visited, not your own <u>stories</u> or history of similar situations.

- Keep the visit <u>short</u>, <u>10</u> minutes maximum unless it is a <u>life</u> threatening situation or the person <u>clearly</u> does not want you to leave.

- Read a <u>short</u> scripture that is <u>appropriate</u> to the situation.

- Ask if there is anything the person <u>needs</u> you to do for them. It is important to <u>follow up</u> on this need. If the person asks you to do something that you know you will not be able to do, it is better to tell them so and ask if there is anything else you can do instead.

- Close the visit with <u>prayer</u>.

Effective and Healthy Pastoral Visits - Student's Worksheet

Effective and healthy pastoral visits include:

- Focus on the _____ being visited, not your own _____ or history of similar situations.

- Keep the visit _____ , _____ minutes maximum unless it is a _____ threatening situation or the person _____ does not want you to leave.

- Read a _____ scripture that is _____ to the situation.

- Ask if there is anything the person _____ you to do for them. It is important to _____ on this need. If the person asks you to do something that you know you will not be able to do, it is better to tell them so and ask if there is anything else you can do instead.

- Close the visit with _____.

Role Play 1 – The Pastor Is Going Out of Town

Man 1: Did you hear about the pastor's granddaughter winning the contest?

Man 2: What contest?

Man 1: She entered a horse riding competition and won first place in her state. Now she has the chance to compete in the national championship. No one thought she would win because she is so young. Now everyone says she is the favorite to win.

Man 2: That's great. I'm sure the pastor is happy.

Man 1: He is very excited. As a matter of fact, he has been trying to figure out how he can go to Kentucky next week to watch her compete.

Man 2: That's wonderful. I hope it will work out for him to go. That is a once in a lifetime experience.

Man 1: I know, but it's short notice. How will he get off work? Who would preach for him next Sunday? What about Mrs. Mapletree's surgery next week? Who would go visit her in the hospital if the pastor is away?

Man 2: Hmmmm … you know, the pastor has made a lot of sacrifices for our church over the years.

Man 1: You're right; he really has.

Man 2: The pastor's boss is my cousin. I bet I could talk him into giving the pastor the time off work to go see his granddaughter.

Man 1: That's a great idea. I think you should do it. I have next Tuesday off work. I could go down to see Mrs. Mapletree after her surgery if only I knew what to say?

Man 2: Surely you can think of something to say; just read a scripture and say a prayer with her.

Man 1: I don't know. I'm not a pastor. I've never been to seminary. What if I don't say the right things?

Man 2: I think God would help you. Why don't you tell the pastor you'll take care of visiting Mrs. Mapletree while he is away?

Man 1: Okay, I'll do it. After all, the pastor has done so much for us. This is a small thing for us to do for him. But what about the sermon? Visiting Mrs. Mapletree is one thing; preaching a sermon is another. I can't do that.

Man 2: Well, who will do it?

Man 1: What about Rev. Sleepy from over in Next Village?

Man 2: We asked him to come last year when the pastor had surgery. But he is so old that he kept falling asleep during the sermon. I don't think he would be a good choice.

Man 1: What about that young fellow who works for the denomination? He seems like he has a lot of energy. Maybe he could come over and preach.

Man 2: Have you seen his website? He's booked until next Christmas. There is no way he'll be able to come on one week's notice.

Man 1: Well, who is going to do it?

Man 2: Hmmmm . . . if only there was a man who really loved God and cared about the pastor enough to help him out in this situation.

Man 1: What about you? You love God. You really care about the pastor. If you volunteer to preach, he can go watch his granddaughter ride her horse in the national competition. You are always talking about how much the pastor needs to take a vacation anyway. You can do it!

Man 2: Me! I'm not a preacher.

Man 1: Well, if I'm going to visit Mrs. Mapletree, you'll have to preach on Sunday.

Man 2: ME! Are you crazy? I can't preach.

Man 1: You've taught Sunday School lots of times; just think of it as a big classroom.

Man 2: Me! I can't preach. I don't have the training. I don't have the skills. I don't have a good suit to wear. I get all tongue-tied when I get nervous. I can't do it.

Man 1: Seems like just last week the pastor preached from Philippians about how we can do all things through Christ who strengthens us. This sounds like one of those things God can do through us if we let Him.

Man 2: Oh, there you go quoting scripture. But you are right; the pastor did preach about that in his last sermon. And it was a good sermon. Maybe if I trust God, He can help me do it.

Man 1: The pastor would love to see his granddaughter. He really does need a vacation anyway.

Man 2: Let me pray about it this afternoon and then let's call the pastor tonight and see what he thinks.

Role Play 2 – The Worst Visit Ever

The pastor will play the role of the person being visited. A student will play the role of the person doing the visiting.

Pastor: Hello, Brother Smith, can I come in for a few minutes and talk to you?

Smith: Actually I'm about to head out to watch my son play baseball. Can I call you tomorrow to set up a better time for you to come by?

Pastor: Oh, it will only take a minute; I'll just come in right now and only stay a short time.

Smith: Well, actually, this really isn't a good time and . . . .

Pastor: Don't worry; I'll just take a minute of your time.

Smith: Ah, okay, sure, come on in.

Pastor: You know my son used to play ball. What position does your son play?

Smith: Well, he is the right fielder and he is . . .

Pastor: Right field, that's not a very important spot. My son was the pitcher. Doesn't your boy know how to work hard?

Smith: Ah, I think he works hard; he's just . . .

Pastor: Oh, that's okay. Not every boy can be a star. By the way, I played ball in school too. I was the highest scorer in the league three years running. Now, if I recall, you weren't much of a sports person yourself, were you.

Smith: No, I was more into academics. You know, pastor, I really need to get going or I'll be late for the game.

Pastor: It's okay, I've just got a few questions I want to ask you about your spiritual condition. You do care about whether you burn in hell or not?

Smith: Well, yes, of course I do; that's why I've been coming to your church lately. It's just that my son's game starts in ten minutes.

Pastor: Ah, ball games, I remember when I was a kid I loved to play ball. I'll have to come by and tell you all about how great I was sometime when I'm not so busy.

Smith: Yes, maybe some other time, but right now I need to get going.

Pastor: Okay, well, let me just read you some scripture. I think one or two chapters from Leviticus might help you think about what is more important in life. Let me get out my Bible and I'll read those two chapters quickly.

Evaluation Form for Session One: Introduction to Preaching and Pastoral Care

Please evaluate the session using the scale below.

Completely Agree (5)   Partially Agree (4)   Neither Agree nor Disagree (3)

Partially Disagree (2)   Completely Disagree (1)

Preaching Segment:

The teacher was prepared for the session.

5   4   3   2   1

Time was used effectively during the session.

5   4   3   2   1

I understand why preaching is important.

5   4   3   2   1

I can explain to someone else why preaching is important.

5   4   3   2   1

I accept that a good sermon begins with scripture.

5   4   3   2   1

I can recall at least three types of sermons.

5   4   3   2   1

The type of sermon I think is most effective is

_____

I believe this because

_____

The most helpful part of this segment was

_____

One suggestion for improving this segment in the future would be

_____

Pastoral Care Segment:

The teacher was prepared for the session.

5   4   3   2   1

Time was used effectively during the session.

5   4   3   2   1

I understand why pastoral care is important.

5   4   3   2   1

I can explain to someone else why pastoral care is important.

5   4   3   2   1

I accept that good pastoral care is people centered.

5   4   3   2   1

I can recall at least two types of pastoral visits.

5   4   3   2   1

The type of visit I would be most comfortable making is

_____

I feel this way because

_____

The most helpful part of this segment was

_____

One suggestion for improving this segment in the future would be

_____

Practical Application Segment:

The teacher was prepared for the session.

5   4   3   2   1

Time was used effectively during the session.

5   4   3   2   1

The role play about the pastor going out of town was helpful.

5   4   3   2   1

The role play about the worst visit ever was helpful.

5   4   3   2   1

I understand my assignment for the next session.

5   4   3   2   1

The most helpful part of this segment was

_____

One suggestion for improving this segment in the future is

_____

Chapter 6

Selecting the Sermon Text and Making Hospital Visits

If lay people are only going to preach on very rare occasions, the selection of the text from which to preach might be based on one of their favorite scriptures. But once lay people begin to preach on a regular basis, it becomes more of a challenge to find a text from which to deliver a sermon that is both fresh, relevant and theological balanced. This session will help lay people who are engaged in regular preaching gain skills in how to select the text for a sermon.

When people are in the hospital, they are often scared, lonely, and in need of encouragement. When they receive a pastoral visit in that time of difficulty, not only does it meet their spiritual need, but a growing body of evidence also suggests that they physically recover faster as well. Therefore learning how to make a good hospital visit is important for lay people who want to help their church minister more effectively.

Session Two Teaching Plan

Welcome and Greeting Time (10 minutes)

- Ask how the week has been.

- Ask if there are any special prayer needs.

- Call on one of the students to open in prayer.

- Review the types of sermons that were presented in the last session.

Learning to Preach Segment (50 minutes)

- Ask those who may have preached before to share how they selected their texts in the past.

- The pastor will share a personal testimony for ten minutes about the challenge of selecting a scripture text for the sermon each week. Feel free to also invite a guest pastor to come share this testimony to give the students a broader perspective.

- The pastor will present a 30-minute lecture on the topic, "Selecting the Sermon Text" using the handout provided. Remind the students that they may wish to purchase William Evan's book, *How to Prepare Sermons*.

- Ask those who brought study books to pass them around. Ask them to share why each book is helpful to them. The pastor should also bring several books to show the class, including a concordance, a commentary and a Bible dictionary. Take time to explain how to use a concordance, a commentary, and a Bible dictionary. Explain the difference between these three key reference books and why they are so important. Point out that a concordance helps a person find verses with certain words in them. A commentary explains what a passage means, often giving historical data and explanations of the original language. A Bible dictionary defines certain terms, names and places that may be less familiar to modern readers but are important in understanding the context of a Bible passage. All three of these types of books are essential for a new preacher in building a balanced sermon. Suggest that the students invest in a copy of each of these three types of books if they do not already own them.

Take a ten-minute break.

Learning to Make Visits Segment (45 minutes)

- Review the keys to effective pastoral visits that were presented in the last session.

- The pastor should share a testimony about a pastoral visit to a patient in a hospital (leaving out names for privacy sake) and what could have been done differently on that visit to make it more effective.

- Lead a twenty-minute guided discussion on "Happy and Effective Hospital Visits." Give the class the handout to take notes with. Have the class members interact with these ideas and discuss one another's responses. Point out the website that the handout was adapted from. Let the students know they may wish to go to the website for additional ideas.

- Discuss the importance of maintaining confidentiality with those being visited.

- Discuss the importance of following health guidelines in medical institutions.

Take a ten-minute break.

Practical Application Segment: (55 minutes)

- "Hospital Visit" role play. Ask two lay people to read a pre-written role play about a good hospital visit. Ask two other lay people to read a pre-written role play about a poor hospital visit.

- Role play evaluation – discuss the differences between the two visits.

- Assignment for the next session: Ask if any of the students have done any preaching before. It is assumed that at least one of them will have. Ask if one that has preached before would be willing to volunteer to preach a one-point fifteen-minute sermon at the next session. If no one has preached before, still ask for a volunteer. Although the group has not yet been taught how to preach, this exercise will reinforce the values of willingness, trust in the Holy Spirit, and practical experience rather than the absolute necessity of formal training.

Session evaluation

- Pass out the evaluation form for this session and ask the group to take 3 minutes to fill it in.

- Ask one of the students to close the session with prayer.

Selecting the Sermon Text – Leader's Guide

Selecting the scripture text from which to preach is very important. Consider these ideas when selecting a text.

Definition and length of the text

- The word "text" is from the Latin "textus" and means something <u>woven</u> or spun. A <u>sermon</u> is literally woven out of the text.

- A text is not just a <u>motto</u>, nor should it be chosen after the theme.

- The text may be long or short, but should cover the <u>complete</u> thought of the original writer.

Advantages of Having a Specific Text for Each Sermon

- It awakens the <u>interest</u> of the audience and grabs their attention.

- It gains the <u>confidence</u> of the audience because they know the preacher will not just be sharing his own opinions.

- It gives the preacher <u>authority</u> and boldness in the proclamation of the message because there is supernatural power in scriptural texts.

- It will keep the preacher's mind from <u>wandering</u> by forcing him to make all his comments around that particular <u>text</u>.

- It will keep the preacher <u>biblical</u> by not allowing him to interject too much human <u>opinion</u> or cultural prejudices into the sermon.

General Principles Regarding the Choice of the Text

- One must carefully consider the <u>spiritual</u> needs of the people to whom one is ministering. What does the congregation <u>need</u> to hear at this moment in their spiritual walk?

- There should be a careful consideration of the <u>cycle</u> of truth preached. Are you preaching the <u>whole</u> counsel of God or just your favorite sections of scripture?

- There should be a careful consideration of one's <u>ability</u> to deal with the text and the subject derived from it. Do you know enough about this subject to offer real <u>insight</u> and applications from the text?

Personal Principles Regarding the Choice of a Text

- The preacher must practice a regular <u>reading</u> of the Word of God. This is of upmost importance before one can preach to <u>others</u>. This does not mean that you use your personal devotions as sermon <u>preparation</u>, but don't be surprised when a sermon <u>evolves</u> out of your personal devotional time.

- The preacher is encouraged to use a <u>notebook</u> or some other record keeping tool so that the preacher can record what the <u>Spirit</u> is saying. These records often become the building <u>blocks</u> of many sermons.

- <u>Reading</u> good Christian books provides rich sermon <u>material</u>.

- Following the <u>guidance</u> of the Holy Spirit is very important.

Important Precautions Regarding the Choice of a Text

- Be careful about using <u>odd</u> texts. Though all scripture is from God, some are <u>easier</u> to preach than others. Some are better suited for a <u>teaching</u> environment. Others are better handled by a <u>scholar</u> in an academic setting.

  Example of a text that has an odd phrase that is complicated to understand:

  1 Corinthians 15:29 – "Else what shall they do which are baptized for the dead, if the dead rise not at all? Why are they then baptized for the dead?" (KJV)

- Don't choose a text that will look <u>ridiculous</u> because of extenuating <u>circumstances</u>.

  For example, imagine an obese pastor preaching from Proverbs 23:2 – "and put a knife to your throat if you are given to gluttony." (KJV)

- Don't choose texts that create <u>expectations</u> which neither the sermon nor preacher can fulfill.

  For example; a topical sermon on how to "divorce proof" your marriage or "guarantee" financial success.

- Don't use <u>questionable</u> texts.

  An example of a text with a questionable meaning is 2 Samuel 12:22-23, "He answered, "While the child was still alive, I fasted and wept. I thought, 'Who knows? The LORD may be gracious to me and let the child live.' But now that he is dead, why should I fast? Can I bring him back again? I will go to him, but he will not return to me." (KJV) Some people think that this verse means that children who die automatically go to heaven. Others absolutely reject that idea. If you are a lay preacher, it might be better to let the pastor deal with such questionable texts because the pastor is the one who will have to do the counseling afterwards if people become confused.

- Don't <u>mutilate</u> a text by only using a <u>part</u> of it out of context.

  For example, Ephesians 5:22 "Wives, submit to your husbands as to the Lord." (KJV)

  This verse must be understood in the context that it was written or else it can be used to justify all manner of abuses toward women.

- Though it is often easier to preach from the New Testament, remember that Old Testament texts should not be <u>neglected</u>.

Above outline adapted from: Evans, William, How to Prepare Sermons (Chicago: Moody Bible Institute, 1964), pages 20-31.

Selecting the Sermon Text – Student's Key

Selecting the scripture text from which to preach is very important. Consider these ideas when selecting a text.

Definition and length of the text

- The word "text" is from the Latin "textus" and means something _____ or spun. A _____ is literally woven out of the text.

- A text is not just a _____, nor should it be chosen after the theme.

- The text may be long or short, but should cover the _____ thought of the original writer.

Advantages of Having a Specific Text for Each Sermon

- It awakens the _____ of the audience and grabs their attention.

- It gains the _____ of the audience because they know the preacher will not just be sharing his own opinions.

- It gives the preacher _____ and boldness in the proclamation of the message because there is supernatural power in scriptural texts.

- It will keep the preacher's mind from _____ by forcing him to make all his comments around that particular _____.

- It will keep the preacher _____ by not allowing him to interject too much human _____ or cultural prejudices into the sermon.

General Principles Regarding the Choice of the Text

- One must carefully consider the _____ needs of the people to whom one is ministering. What does the congregation _____ to hear at this moment in their spiritual walk?

- There should be a careful consideration of the _____ of truth preached. Are you preaching the _____ counsel of God or just your favorite sections of scripture?

- There should be a careful consideration of one's _____ to deal with the text and the subject derived from it. Do you know enough about this subject to offer real _____ and applications from the text?

Personal Principles Regarding the Choice of a Text

- The preacher must practice a regular _____ of the Word of God. This is of upmost importance before one can preach to _____. This does not mean that you use your personal devotions as sermon _____, but don't be surprised when a sermon _____ out of your personal devotional time.

- The preacher is encouraged to use a _____ or some other record keeping tool so that the preacher can record what the _____ is saying. These records often become the building _____ of many sermons.

- _____ good Christian books provides rich sermon _____.

- Following the _____ of the Holy Spirit is very important.

Important Precautions Regarding the Choice of a Text

- Be careful about using _____ texts. Though all scripture is from God, some are _____ to preach than others. Some are better suited for a _____ environment. Others are better handled by a _____ in an academic setting.

  Example of a text that has an odd phrase that is complicated to understand:

  1 Corinthians 15:29 – "Else what shall they do which are baptized for the dead, if the dead rise not at all? Why are they then baptized for the dead?" (KJV)

- Don't choose a text that will look _____ because of extenuating _____.

  For example, imagine an obese pastor preaching from Proverbs 23:2 – "and put a knife to your throat if you are given to gluttony." (KJV)

- Don't choose texts that create _____ which neither the sermon nor preacher can fulfill.

  For example, a topical sermon on how to "divorce proof" your marriage or "guarantee" financial success.

- Don't use _____ texts.

  An example of a text with a questionable meaning is 2 Samuel 12:22-23, "He answered, "While the child was still alive, I fasted and wept. I thought, 'Who knows? The LORD may be gracious to me and let the child live.' But now that he is dead, why should I fast? Can I bring him back again? I will go to him, but he will not return to me." (KJV) Some people think that this verse means that children who die automatically go to heaven. Others absolutely reject that idea. If you are a lay preacher, it might be better to let the pastor deal with such questionable texts because the pastor is the one who will have to do the counseling afterwards if people become confused.

- Don't _____ a text by only using a _____ of it out of context.

  For example, Ephesians 5:22 "Wives, submit to your husbands as to the Lord." (KJV)

  This verse must be understood in the context that it was written or else it can be used to justify all manner of abuses toward women.

- Though it is often easier to preach from the New Testament, remember that ___ Testament texts should not be _____.

Above outline adapted from: Evans, William, How to Prepare Sermons (Chicago: Moody Bible Institute, 1964), pages 20-31.

Happy and Effective Hospital Visits - Leader's Key

By following these suggestions, your visit with a hospital patient should be happier and more effective.

1. Do not wear <u>cologne</u>. <u>Cologne</u> can gag even healthy people.

2. Leave the <u>gum</u> at home. No one likes to listen to people <u>chew</u> and smack <u>gum</u>.

3. Always check with the <u>nurse</u> before you bring <u>food</u> to a patient, even if the patient asks you for it. It might be a detriment to the patient's condition.

4. If you do take a gift of food, please, do not <u>eat</u> any of it. Remember it is for the patient. And of course don't eat the patient's <u>food</u>, either from his tray or from the gifts others have left.

5. When you greet the patient, if it is physically feasible, take his or her hand <u>gently</u>. Never <u>hug</u>. Most people do not like to be touched when they are sick, especially if they have had <u>surgery</u>.

6. Be polite and <u>stand</u> if there are not enough chairs. You're only going to be there a short time.

7. Never <u>sit</u> on the <u>bed</u>; it cramps the patient. If there is a <u>second</u> bed in the room, do not sit on it, even if it is not being used. The staff may have it ready for a <u>new</u> patient and may not have time to <u>freshen</u> it up before a new patient needs it.

8. Talk <u>audibly</u>, not too softly or too loudly. Increase your <u>volume</u> if you find the patient cannot hear you. Sometimes, when people are sick, their minds are a bit <u>fuzzy</u> from pills and pain.

9. Only stay a few <u>minutes</u>. The point of your visit is to wish the patient well, not to spend a long period of time with him or her. <u>Extended</u> visits often <u>tire</u> a patient more than he or she realizes.

10. If you take a <u>gift</u>, make sure that your gift is appropriate for the <u>situation</u>. For example, if the patient has just had eye surgery, then he or she won't be able to read a book.

11. Only talk about <u>happy</u> situations, not about <u>bad</u> news. Never talk about your own <u>past</u> illnesses or operations.

12. If there are <u>relatives</u> present, say a quick hello, leave your gift, wish the patient a <u>speedy</u> recovery, and then leave. The relatives will want quality time and <u>privacy</u> with the patient. Sometimes they come from quite a <u>distance</u>. They may not be able to come back soon, but you can always return at a later time.

13. If either the <u>nurse</u> or doctor enters the room to do something for the patient, be polite and <u>leave</u> the room while they are attending the patient. Do this even if the patient says it is okay for you stay.

14. If the patient wants to go for a <u>walk</u> with you, check with the <u>nurse</u> first. The same would be true if the patient asks you for assistance in getting out of <u>bed</u> or in using the bathroom.

15. If you don't know how to <u>respond</u> to something the patient says, sometimes it is better to say <u>nothing</u> at all. Just express your <u>concern</u>, offer a prayer, and graciously make your departure.

16. Remember that patients are in the hospital because they are sick. Use <u>common</u> sense, <u>smile</u>, and be <u>positive</u> during the visit. If you become upset, just excuse yourself until you can regain control of your own <u>emotions</u>. Be aware that conversations in the hall can be overheard. The whole point of visiting patients in the hospital is to cheer them up. So don't do anything to make the situation <u>tenser</u> than it already is.

Adapted from the website:
http://www.essortment.com/all/hospitaletiqu_reny.htm, accessed September 27, 2008.

Happy and Effective Hospital Visits – Student's Worksheet

By following these suggestions, your visit with a hospital patient should be happier and more effective.

1. Do not wear _____. _____ can gag even healthy people.

2. Leave the _____ at home. No one likes to listen to people _____ and smack _____.

3. Always check with the _____ before you bring _____ to a patient, even if the patient asks you for it. It might be a detriment to the patient's condition.

4. If you do take a gift of food, please, do not _____ any of it. Remember it is for the patient. And of course don't eat the patient's _____, either from his tray or from the gifts others have left.

5. When you greet the patient, if it is physically feasible, take his or her hand _____. Never _____. Most people do not like to be touched when they are sick, especially if they have had _____.

6. Be polite and _____ if there are not enough chairs. You're only going to be there a short time.

7. Never _____ on the _____; it cramps the patient. If there is a _____ bed in the room, do not sit on it, even if it is not being used. The staff may have it ready for a _____ patient and may not have time to _____ it up before a new patient needs it.

8. Talk _____, not too softly or too loudly. Increase your _____ if you find the patient cannot hear you. Sometimes, when people are sick, their minds are a bit _____ from pills and pain.

9. Only stay a few _____. The point of your visit is to wish the patient well not to spend a long period of time with him or her. _____ visits often _____ a patient more than he or she realizes.

10. If you take a _____, make sure that your gift is appropriate for the _____. For example, if the patient has just had eye surgery then he or she won't be able to read a book.

11. Only talk about _____ situations, not about _____ news. Never talk about your own _____ illnesses or operations.

12. If there are _____ present, say a quick hello, leave your gift and wish the patient a _____ recovery and then leave. The relatives will want quality time and _____ with the patient. Sometimes they come from quite a _____. They may not be able to come back soon, but you can always return later.

13. If either the _____ or doctor enters the room to do something for the patient, be polite and _____ the room while they are attending the patient. Do this even if the patient says it is okay for you stay.

14. If the patient wants to go for a _____ with you, check with the _____ first. The same would be true if the patient asks you for assistance in getting out of _____ or in using the bathroom.

15. If you don't know how to _____ to something the patient says, sometimes it is better to say _____ at all. Just express your _____, offer a prayer and graciously make your departure.

16. Remember that patients are in the hospital because they are sick. Use _____ sense, _____ and be _____ during the visit. If you become upset, just excuse yourself until you can regain control of your own _____. Be aware that conversations in the _____ can be overheard. The whole point of visiting patients in the hospital is to cheer them up. So don't do anything to make the situation _____ than it already is.

Adapted from the website:
http://www.essortment.com/all/hospitaletiqu_reny.htm, accessed September 27, 2008.

Role Play 3 – Hospital Visits: Good and Poor

A good hospital visit might look like this.

Visitor: Hello, Brother Smith. I wanted to stop in and say hello for a minute and pray with you. Is that okay?

Patient: Yes, please do. I've been so lonely and worried while I've been in the hospital and I really need the prayer.

Visitor: We have been praying for you at church.

Patient: Thank you. I received the lovely flowers from the Sunday School class, that really made my day.

Visitor: Is there anything we can do at the house for you while you are in the hospital? I can send one of the teenage boys by to cut the grass and my wife can collect the mail and newspapers for you if you would like us to.

Patient: The grass was pretty high when the ambulance brought me to the hospital. If one of the boys cut the grass, it would be wonderful. My cousin is collecting the mail and papers for me, but thanks for offering.

Visitor: Would you like me to read you a scripture before I pray for you?

Patient: Yes, that would be a blessing.

Visitor: Do you have a favorite scripture you want me to read?

Patient: I always feel comforted when I hear Psalm 23; how about that one?

Visitor: Okay, and then I'll say a prayer for you and let you rest.

Patient: Thanks so much for coming by.

A poor hospital visit might look like this.

Visitor: Hello, Brother Smith. I wanted to stop in and see if you were going to make it. I heard you were real bad off.

Patient: Ah, yes, it has been a rough few days.

Visitor: From what the ladies said at church, the doctors don't give you much hope.

Patient: Well, they have said that my chances are not as good as they had hoped.

Visitor: You know my cousin Tom had the same thing and he suffered for months and months before he finally died. But he was a Christian so we knew he went to heaven, so it was okay.

Patient: Well, I am a Christian; I came to know the Lord ten years ago, so I guess I'll be okay if I don't make it.

Visitor: Well, I hope you are a Christian. But if you've ever doubted it, now would be the time to make it right. Can I share the Romans Road with you?

Patient: Well, I guess, but I'm kind of tired; maybe you can come back later.

Visitor: Don't you want to hear the Gospel? It's what you need most of all, especially if you are doubting your salvation.

Patient: I do not doubt my salvation, but I am worried about how my wife and kids will get by if I die.

Visitor: I'm sure they can get welfare; the state won't let them starve.

Patient: Ah, well, I guess that's reassuring. Thanks so much for coming by. I think I need to rest now.

Visitor: Okay, well, it was good to see you, and I'll tell everyone all about your situation so they'll know just how bad it is. That way they can pray better about it.

Evaluation Form for Session Two: Selecting the Sermon Text and Making Hospital Visits

Please evaluate the session using the scale below.

Completely Agree (5)   Partially Agree (4)   Neither Agree nor Disagree (3)

Partially Disagree (2)   Completely Disagree (1)

Preaching Segment:

The teacher was prepared for the session.

5   4   3   2   1

Time was used effectively during the session.

5   4   3   2   1

I understand the value of intentional advanced planning in selecting a text.

5   4   3   2   1

I understand how to select a sermon text.

5   4   3   2   1

I can explain to someone else at least two ways to study the text.

5   4   3   2   1

The method of study that I think will be most helpful to me is

_____

I believe this because

_____

The most helpful part of this segment was

_____

One suggestion for improving this segment in the future would be

_____

Pastoral Care Segment:

The teacher was prepared for the session.

5   4   3   2   1

Time was used effectively during the session.

5   4   3   2   1

I understand the basics of what I should say when making a hospital visit.

5   4   3   2   1

I see the value of avoiding saying certain things when making a hospital visit.

5   4   3   2   1

The best way to end the visit is with prayer.

5   4   3   2   1

The most significant aspect of making a hospital visit is

_____

I feel this way because

_____

The most helpful part of this segment was

_____

One suggestion for improving this segment in the future would be

_____

Practical Application Segment:

The teacher was prepared for the session.

5   4   3   2   1

Time was used effectively during the session.

5   4   3   2   1

The role play about the hospital visit was helpful.

5   4   3   2   1

I understand my assignment for the next session.

5   4   3   2   1

The most helpful part of this segment was

_____

One suggestion for improving this segment in the future is

_____

Chapter 7

Strengthening Sermon Preparation, Presenting the Sermon and Making Absentee Visits

The strength of a good sermon lies in the preparation. Though experience is its own teacher, sermon preparation will go more smoothly when a new preacher learns to use certain skills correctly. Once the sermon is prepared, then it must be delivered in a way that catches the attention of the congregation. Many good sermons fall flat because of poor delivery. Though nothing can replace the power of the Holy Spirit, good rhetorical skills are important for effective preaching. This chapter will help lay people think through ways to prepare and deliver a good sermon.

People go through phases in life. As they move through those phases, sometimes they stray from church. It might have started as a short absence due to an illness, or perhaps a change in work schedule, but the more time that goes by, the easier it is for a short term absentee to become a long term absentee. A well timed and uplifting visit from a caring lay person can help an absentee know they are missed and encourage them to return to church. This chapter will train lay people to make such visits.

Session Three Teaching Plan

Welcome and Greeting Time (10 minutes)

- Ask the students how their week has been and if there are any special prayer needs.

- Call on one of the students to open in prayer.

- Review the previous session by asking why it is important to have a specific scripture text for each sermon.

Learning to Preach Segment (1 hour and 15 minutes)

- Give a thirty minute lecture entitled "Strengthening Sermon Preparation" using the handout. Suggest to the students that they may want to purchase Wayne McDill's book, *Twelve Essentials for Good Preaching*, as a resource for further study.

- Follow up with a discussion on "How to Present a Strong Sermon" using the handout.

- The pastor should share a personal testimony regarding which presentation methods are the easiest for him to use personally and which are the hardest.

- Ask the class to think about opportunities they have had to preach. What presentation methods were easiest or hardest for them? Discuss the responses.

- Lead a discussion about the question, "Why Should We Use Variety in Our Preaching?" Use the handout to incorporate into the discussion some of the ways that adults learn.

Take a ten-minute break.

Learning to Make Visits Segment (45 minutes)

- Review the previous session by asking, "What are the key elements to a happy and effective hospital visit?"

- Use the handout to give an overview of how to make an effective absentee visit.

- The pastor should share a testimony about a recent absentee visit and how it impacted the life of the person being visited.

Take a ten-minute break.

Practical Application Segment (50 minutes)

- "Absentee Visit" role play 1 - Model a good absentee visit using a role play. In the role play, the pastor will play the role of the pastor. One student should act as the pastor's assistant and another student should act as the absentee. The pastor should have told the "absentee" privately in advance to respond positively to the visit.

- "Absentee Visit" role play 2 - Then ask the student who was assisting the pastor to act out the role play again. In this scenario, the other student will act as the pastor's assistant while the pastor serves as the absentee. The pastor will pretend to be less positive in response to the visit. Be mindful not to be too harsh, just act less than enthusiastic about the visit so that the person making the visit can feel what it is like to be rejected on an absentee visit.

- Role play evaluation - Discuss how it felt when the first absentee responded positively. Discuss how it felt when the second absentee responded less positively. Discuss how a person never knows how someone will respond to a visit. Discuss the need to be careful in how one reacts to negative responses.

- One-point mini-sermon: Ask the pre-selected student to preach the sample sermon.

- Sermon evaluation: Explain that the purpose of evaluation is not to make a person feel bad about perceived weaknesses, nor to make a student boast about perceived strengths. The purpose of the evaluation is to help each person understand the experience so they can improve and grow in preaching abilities and styles.

Assignments for the next session

- Ask for a volunteer to preach a one-point fifteen-minute sermon at the next session. It needs to be someone other than the person who preached at today's session.

- The pastor shall also take each student on an absentee visit before the next session. The pastor will guide this visit and the lay people will observe. The experience will be discussed during the next session.

Session Evaluation

- Pass out the evaluation form for this session and ask the group to take three minutes to fill it in.

- Ask a student to close the session with prayer.

Strengthening Sermon Preparation Skills – Leader's Key

- Our <u>approach</u> to the text will involve <u>inductive</u> Bible study. Inductive Bible study is when you give careful examination of all the <u>details</u> of what the <u>original</u> writer intended to say before drawing a <u>conclusion</u> about the meaning of the text. You begin with the <u>parts</u> and move to the <u>whole</u>, as opposed to starting with the whole and then examining the parts.

- Our method for getting from the text to the sermon is the <u>key</u> <u>word</u> method. This method allows the preacher to focus on key words that will <u>explain</u> the text piece by piece, slowly building an <u>understanding</u> of the whole text.

- As we do inductive Bible study, we begin to discover the biblical writer's intended <u>theological</u> meaning in the text. We do this by a careful analysis of all <u>facets</u> of the text. Only by understanding the theological meaning will we then be able to offer appropriate <u>application</u> of the text to the audience.

- Give careful consideration of the <u>context</u> in which the text was originally written. Knowing the context means understanding what is said <u>before</u> and <u>after</u> the text. It also means understanding the <u>history</u>, local <u>culture</u>, economic <u>conditions</u>, and <u>geographical</u> facts. These are not just <u>extra</u> bits of knowledge; they are often the key to <u>fully</u> understanding why the author wrote what he did.

- Seek to <u>influence</u> the audience through the use of the rhetorical <u>elements</u> common to persuasion.

- Aim for a <u>response</u> of faith and <u>obedience</u> to the biblical truth on the part of the audience. Remember that you cannot <u>force</u> the audience to respond; you can only aim for a response.

- Remember that sermon preparation is a <u>supernatural</u> endeavor. You must be <u>prayed</u> up and <u>confessed</u> up, as well as <u>studied</u> up.

- Remember that the great weakness of preaching is <u>fuzzy</u>, ill defined <u>ideas</u>. If you have not <u>thought</u> it out completely for yourself, you probably won't be able to <u>explain</u> it well to others.

- Expository preaching allows the text to <u>shape</u> the sermon. Dig into the text. Analyze the parts and let the whole slowly <u>form</u> in your heart and mind. Even if you are using a type of sermon other than expository, still let the scripture fully grip your own heart before preaching it to others.

- Pick a <u>legitimate</u> text. The original <u>writer</u> wrote the text in units of <u>thought</u>; follow them as closely as you can and you will have a <u>stronger</u> sermon.

Above outline adapted from: McDill, Wayne, Twelve Essential Skills for Great Preaching (Nashville: B & H Publishing Group, 3006), pages 3-17.

Strengthening Sermon Preparation Skills – Student Worksheet

- Our _____ to the text will involve _____ Bible study. Inductive Bible study is when you give careful examination of all the _____ of what the _____ writer intended to say before drawing a _____ about the meaning of the text. You begin with the _____ and move to the _____, as opposed to starting with the whole and then examining the parts.

- Our method for getting from the text to the sermon is the _____ method. This method allows the preacher to focus on key words that will _____ the text piece by piece, slowly building an _____ of the whole text.

- As we do inductive Bible study, we begin to discover the biblical writer's intended _____ meaning in the text. We do this by a careful analysis of all _____ of the text. Only by understanding the theological meaning will we then be able to offer appropriate _____ of the text to the audience.

- Give careful consideration of the _____ in which the text was originally written. Knowing the context means understanding what is said _____ and _____ the text. It also means understanding the _____, local _____, economic _____ and _____ facts. These are not just _____ bits of knowledge, they are often the key to _____ understanding why the author wrote what he did.

- Seek to _____ the audience through the use of the rhetorical _____ common to persuasion.

- Aim for a _____ of faith and _____ to the biblical truth on the part of the audience. Remember that you cannot _____ the audience to respond, you can only aim for a response.

- Remember that sermon preparation is a _____ endeavor. You must be _____ up and _____ up, as well as _____ up.

- Remember that the great weakness of preaching is _____, ill defined _____. If you have not _____ it out completely for yourself, you probably won't be able to _____ it well to others.

- Expository preaching allows the text to _____ the sermon. Dig into the text. Analyze the parts and let the whole slowly _____ in your heart and mind. Even if you are using a type of sermon other than expository, still let the scripture fully grip your own heart before preaching it to others.

- Pick a _____ text. The original _____ wrote the text in units of _____, follow them as closely as you can and you will have a _____ sermon.

Above outline adapted from: McDill, Wayne, Twelve Essential Skills for Great Preaching (Nashville: B & H Publishing Group, 3006), pages 3-17.

How to Deliver a Strong Sermon – Leader's Key

- Have a strong <u>central</u> thesis that can be <u>easily</u> communicated to the audience. Communicate it <u>early</u> and often.

- Use facts, dates, figures or other <u>objective</u> points of information that can be <u>verified</u> by others. This gives <u>credibility</u> to the sermon and shows that you know your subject well. <u>Document</u> those sources if it is appropriate.

- Make sure your sources are <u>reliable</u>. Don't use commentaries or study Bibles that are known to contain <u>incorrect</u> material or poor translation/interpretation techniques.

- Double check your flow of <u>logic</u> for loopholes or gaps. Then correct the <u>weak</u> points before you present the sermon.

- Use your <u>body</u> language and tone of <u>voice</u> to project the right message at the right time.

- Make sure you articulate <u>clearly</u> and <u>pronounce</u> words correctly. Otherwise you will quickly lose the audience's attention. They may even conclude you do not know what you are talking about and that has <u>serious</u> long term implications for a preacher.

- Don't be afraid to show genuine <u>emotion</u> in appropriate ways and at appropriate times.

- <u>Practice</u> your sermon out loud. Even though the sermon may change some during the actual presentation, hearing yourself <u>speak</u> the words will make you more confident. It will also help you realize what the <u>length</u> of the sermon will most likely be. You can then make adjustments beforehand.

How to Deliver a Strong Sermon – Student Worksheet

- Have a strong _____ thesis that can be _____ communicated to the audience. Communicate it _____ and often.

- Use facts, dates, figures or other _____ points of information that can be _____ by others. This gives _____ to the sermon and shows that you know your subject well. _____ those sources if it is appropriate.

- Make sure your sources are _____. Don't use commentaries or study Bibles that are known to contain _____ material or poor translation/interpretation techniques.

- Double check your flow of _____ for loopholes or gaps. Then correct the _____ points before you present the sermon.

- Use your _____ language and tone of _____ to project the right message at the right time.

- Make sure you articulate _____ and _____ words correctly. Otherwise you will quickly lose the audience's attention. They may even conclude you do not know what you are talking about and that has _____ long term implications for a preacher.

- Don't be afraid to show genuine _____ in appropriate ways and at appropriate times.

- _____ your sermon out loud. Even though the sermon may change some during the actual presentation, hearing yourself _____ the words will make you more confident. It will also help you realize what the _____ of the sermon will most likely be. You can then make adjustments beforehand.

Why Use A Variety of Preaching Methods? – Leader's Key

Though a sermon, by its very nature, is primarily a <u>lecture</u>, preachers should endeavor to use some <u>variety</u> in their sermon delivery. People learn in <u>different</u> ways and what helps one person learn may not help another. In a classroom <u>teaching</u> environment, there are dozens of teaching methods that might be used. In the church setting in which a sermon is normally delivered, there may be fewer options available, but variety can still be effectively utilized.

The three primary learning styles to remember are:

Auditory – These learners <u>listen</u> carefully and comprehend the <u>spoken</u> word easily. You might say their motto is "<u>tell</u> me." These are the learners who gain the most from a traditional sermon that is delivered via lecture method.

Visual – These learners rely on <u>pictures</u> to help them learn. You might say their motto is "<u>show</u> me." They will enjoy a graph, diagram, chart, or other such visual aids that help them "see" what is being talked about. These are the learners who gain the most when a preacher uses a power point presentation, provides a <u>handout</u>, or uses an <u>object</u> lesson as a part of his sermon.

Kinesthetic – These are the learners who need to do something <u>physically</u>. You might say their motto is "let <u>me</u> do it." They want to get out of their seat and take part in the learning <u>experience</u>. These are the learners who gain the most when asked to give a testimony or sing a piece of special music that illustrates the truth of the sermon. They also learn more when the preacher asks the congregation a question for which he wants a verbal response, or when the congregation quotes something together. They are often more moved by some of the <u>liturgical</u> aspects of worship, such as taking communion or lighting candles.

A key concept to remember when preaching to adults is that they want to know "<u>WHY</u>" and "SO WHAT." Often our sermons contain theological truths but fail to explain why that truth is relevant in daily life. Seek to think of ways to make the truth come alive.

Why Use A Variety of Preaching Methods? - Student's Worksheet

Though a sermon, by its very nature, is primarily a _____, preachers should endeavor to use some _____ in their sermon delivery. People learn in _____ ways and what helps one person learn may not help another. In a classroom _____ environment there are dozens of teaching methods that might be used. In the church setting in which a sermon is normally delivered, there may be fewer options available, but variety can still be effectively utilized.

The three primary learning styles to remember are:

Auditory – These learners _____ carefully and comprehend the _____ word easily. You might say their motto is "_____ me." These are the learners who gain the most from a traditional sermon that is delivered via lecture method.

Visual – These learners rely on _____ to help them learn. You might say their motto is "_____ me." They will enjoy a graph, diagram, chart or other such visual aids that help them "see" what is being talked about. These are the learners who gain the most when a preacher uses a power point presentation, provides a _____, or uses an _____ lesson as a part of his sermon.

Kinesthetic – These are the learners who need to do something _____. You might say their motto is "let _____ do it." They want to get out of their seat and take part in the learning _____. These are the learners who gain the most when they are asked to give a testimony or sing a piece of special music that illustrates the truth of the sermon. They also learn more when the preacher asks the congregation a question for which he wants a verbal response, or when the congregation quotes something together. They are often more moved by some of the _____ aspects of worship, such as taking communion or lighting candles.

A key concept to remember when preaching to adults is that they want to know "_____" and "SO WHAT." Often our sermons contain theological truths but fail to explain why that truth is _____ in daily life. Seek to think of ways to make the truth come alive.

Effective Absentee Visits – Leader's Key

The person being visited may not necessarily be an official <u>member</u> of the church, or even be genuinely born again, but they have come enough that they think of your church as "<u>their</u>" church and your congregation thinks of them as part of the "<u>group</u>." If a person has never attended your church or has only come one or two times, you might take different approaches than the steps suggested below.

- Have someone designated to keep an ongoing <u>list</u> of people who have been absent for <u>3</u> weeks or more. If a person misses longer than that without anyone noticing, it will be much more difficult to get them to re-engage in the life of the church.

- Pray to God for the <u>courage</u> to go visit them and the <u>wisdom</u> to respond to whatever they may say. Pray that the individual will receive the visit with <u>joy</u>.

- Make an appointment if the visit will be at the person's <u>home</u>. If you plan to stop by their place of <u>employment</u>, make sure you do not create a situation that will cause them difficulties with their supervisor. It is also possible to turn a causal encounter in the <u>community</u> into an opportunity for a pastoral visit if one is sensitive to the <u>Spirit</u> and <u>looking</u> for such opportunities.

- Remember that your motive is to express <u>concern</u> and let them know they have been <u>missed</u> at church. Though difficult issues may come up in the conversation, the primary motive of an absentee visit is not to "fix a <u>problem</u>." If significant issues come up, then schedule a <u>longer</u> period of time at some later date to discuss those issues with the person instead of making the pastoral visit a protracted one. The obvious exception would be if they have told you in <u>advance</u> that they have significant <u>issues</u> and want to talk specifically about them during the visit.

- Before you visit someone about coming back to church, make sure you first have invited them into "<u>your</u> <u>life</u>." Perhaps invite them to lunch first or to attend a concert or play together. Make a <u>personal</u> connection with them instead of just <u>condemning</u> them for not coming to church. They may have a legitimate <u>reason</u> for not coming. Find out what that reason is and see if you can help resolve it.

- During the visit seek to answer any <u>questions</u> that may come up. Maybe something happened during a worship service that they did not <u>understand</u>. This may have made them hesitant about coming back.

- Offer to <u>sit</u> with them when they come back to church. They may feel less self conscious than just showing up again and sitting alone.

- Let other people at church know you have <u>reached</u> out to the absentee and that they may be <u>returning</u> to church. Encourage others to warmly <u>welcome</u> the person back when he or she arrives.

- Be <u>persistent</u>. Many people have filled their lives with other things and it may take time for them to readjust their <u>schedule</u> enough to find time to come to church. Others have significant emotional or spiritual <u>baggage</u> they are dealing with and it may take a while for them to work through it and be comfortable coming to church. Extend <u>repeated</u> invitations over a period of time without being pushy at any particular point.

- Be the person's <u>friend</u>, whether they return to church or not. People go through <u>phases</u> in life, and sometimes they are more open to spirituality than other times. They will remember who showed real <u>friendship</u> to them and when the time is right they will return to church.

Effective Absentee Visits - Student's Worksheet

The person being visited may not necessarily be an official _____ of the church, or even be genuinely born again, but they have come enough that they think of your church as "_____" church and your congregation thinks of them as part of the "_____." If a person has never attended your church, or has only come one or two times, you might take different approaches than the steps suggested below.

- Have someone designated to keep an ongoing _____ of people who have been absent for _____ weeks or more. If a person misses longer than that without anyone noticing, it will be much more difficult to get them to reengage in the life of the church.

- Pray to God for the _____ to go visit them and the _____ to respond to whatever they may say. Pray that the individual will receive the visit with _____.

- Make an appointment if the visit will be at the person's _____. If you plan to stop by their place of _____, make sure you do not create a situation that will cause them difficulties with their supervisor. It is also possible to turn a causal encounter in the _____ into an opportunity for a pastoral visit if one is sensitive to the _____ and _____ for such opportunities.

- Remember that your motive is to express _____ and let them know they have been _____ at church. Though difficult issues may come up in the conversation, the primary motive of an absentee visit is not to "fix a _____." If significant issues come up, then schedule a _____ period of time at some later date to discuss those issues with the person instead of making the pastoral visit a protracted one. The obvious exception would be if they have told you in _____ that they have significant _____ and want to talk specifically about them during the visit.

- Before you visit someone about coming back to church, make sure you first have invited them into "_____." Perhaps invite them to lunch first or to attend a concert or play together. Make a _____ connection with them instead of just _____ them for not coming to church. They may have a legitimate _____ for not coming. Find out what that reason is and see if you can help resolve it.

- During the visit seek to answer any _____ that may come up. Maybe something happened during a worship service that they did not _____. This may have made them hesitant about coming back.

- Offer to _____ with them when they come back to church. They may feel less self conscious than just showing up again and sitting alone.

- Let other people at church know you have _____ out to the absentee and that they may be _____ to church. Encourage others to warmly _____ the person back when he or she arrives.

- Be _____. Many people have filled their lives with other things and it may take time for them to readjust their _____ enough to find time to come to church. Others have significant emotional or spiritual _____ they are dealing with and it may take a while for them to work through it and be comfortable coming to church.

Extend _____ invitations over a period of time without being pushy at any particular point.

- Be the person's _____, whether they return to church or not. People go through _____ in life and sometimes they are more open to spirituality than other times. They will remember who showed real _____ to them and when the time is right they will return to church.

Role Play – Absentee Visits

Unlike our other role plays, these two are not pre-written. The reason they are not pre-written is to help demonstrate that the principles of a good visit have actually been comprehended by the learners. Break the group up into teams of three. The pastor will be on one of the teams. Give the students five minutes to discuss how they will create a role play of a good visit. The role play itself should last 5 minutes.

The pastor's team should go first and model a good absentee visit using the principles that have been taught. In the role play, have one student be the pastor's assistant and another student act as the absentee.

After the pastor's team has presented the first role play, ask the other teams to do their role plays. If there are not enough students for multiple teams, then the student who was acting as the assistant to the pastor in the first role play will go through the role play again and model a good absentee visit while the pastor acts as the absentee.

Repeat this process as needed to reinforce the main points of a good absentee visit.

Evaluation Form for Session Three: Strengthening Sermon Preparation, Presenting the Sermon and Making Absentee Visits

Please evaluate the session using the scale below.

Completely Agree (5)   Partially Agree (4)   Neither Agree nor Disagree (3)

Partially Disagree (2)   Completely Disagree (1)

Preaching Segment:

The teacher was prepared for the session.

5   4   3   2   1

Time was used effectively during the session.

5   4   3   2   1

I can identify at least two ways to present a sermon.

5   4   3   2   1

I can explain to someone else why it is important to use various methods of preaching.

5   4   3   2   1

I have confidence that I can learn to use a variety of preaching methods.

5   4   3   2   1

The preaching method I think I will be most comfortable with is

_____

I believe this because

_____

The most helpful part of this segment was

_____

One suggestion for improving this segment in the future would be

_____

Pastoral Care Segment:

The teacher was prepared for the session.

5   4   3   2   1

Time was used effectively during the session.

5   4   3   2   1

I understand the basics of what I should say when making an absentee visit.

5   4   3   2   1

I see the value of avoiding saying certain things when making an absentee visit.

5   4   3   2   1

I can think of two ways to end this type of visit effectively.

5   4   3   2   1

The most significant aspect of making an absentee visit is

_____

I feel this way because

_____

The most helpful part of this segment was

_____

One suggestion for improving this segment in the future would be

_____

Practical Application Segment:

The teacher was prepared for the session.

5   4   3   2   1

Time was used effectively during the session.

5   4   3   2   1

The role play about the absentee visit was helpful.

5   4   3   2   1

The sermon preached by my classmate was a helpful example of what we learned in class.

5   4   3   2   1

I understand my assignment for the next session.

5   4   3   2   1

The most helpful part of this segment was

_____

One suggestion for improving this segment in the future is

_____

Chapter 8

How to Conclude a Sermon Well and Make Crisis Visits

Learning to conclude a sermon well is both a science and an art. It is like science because there are some specific ways that a preacher can plan to conclude a sermon that will be conducive to the learners being impacted by that sermon over the long term. It is like art from the perspective that sometimes a preacher may plan to conclude a sermon in one way, but in the circumstance of the moment, it becomes obvious that the sermon should instead be concluded in a different way. Learning to listen to the Holy Spirit and read the responsiveness of the congregation during the sermon will allow a preacher to know which way a sermon should be concluded. This chapter will help equip a preacher with a variety of ways in which a sermon might be concluded for maximum effectiveness.

Members of the pastoral care team may be called upon during a crisis to make a pastoral visit for which there is no real time to prepare. Often crisis situations have a high level of confusion and anxiety and the pastoral visit brings a sense of calmness to what may be a chaotic situation. Learning to make an effective crisis visit will be important to the overall health of a pastoral ministry team. This chapter will give members of the pastoral leadership team the tools by which they may prepare themselves for whatever crisis may arise in the life of the congregation.

Session Four Teaching Plan

Welcome and Greeting Time (10 minutes)

- The pastor should ask the students how the week has been and if there are any special prayer needs.

- The pastor should call on one of the students to open in prayer.

- Review the ways to deliver a strong sermon that were taught in the last session.

- Ask why it is important to use a variety of sermon delivery methods.

Learning to Preach Segment (60 minutes)

- Share two personal examples of a good sermon ending and one example of a poor sermon ending. Show how these endings impacted the effectiveness of the sermons themselves.

- Present a lecture on the necessity and importance of a strong sermon ending. Use the handout that shows the different ways to conclude a sermon. If possible, invite a fellow pastor or two to come and share their own insights on how to conclude a sermon well.

Take a ten-minute break.

Learning to Make Visits Segment (50 minutes)

- Review the principles of how to make a good absentee visit that were taught in the last session.

- Give a 20-minute overview of how to make an effective crisis visit using the outline and worksheet provided on "How to Handle a Crisis Visit."

- Lead a guided discussion with the students on legal issues about crisis visits that need to be reported to the authorities. It might be wise to invite someone who is more knowledgeable on this subject to visit the class and lead this portion of the session.

Take a ten-minute break.

Practical Application Segment (1 hour)

- Call for oral reports on the visits that were made by the lay people since the last session.

- Discuss the following questions: How did the visit work out? What did the lay people learn? The pastor should feel free to share how having the lay people along on the visit impacted the visit. Discuss what changes should be made so future visits will be more effective.

- "Crisis Visit" role play 1 - The pastor will use a role play to model an effective visit to a family who has just experienced an unexpected death. Ask two of the students to act as various members of the family.

- "Crisis Visit" role play 2 - Have one of the students model an effective visit to a man who has just lost his job and is facing serious financial repercussions.

- Role play evaluation – lead a discussion to evaluate the role plays and discuss what was learned through them.

- One-point mini-sermon: Ask the pre-selected student to preach the sample sermon.

- Sermon evaluation: lead a time of evaluation of the sermon just heard. Remind the group that the purpose of evaluation is to help the preacher grow in preaching skills.

Assignments for the next session

- Ask for a volunteer to preach a one-point fifteen-minute sermon at the next session. It needs to be someone other than the person who preached at today's session.

- Ask for a volunteer who might be willing to share in the next session about a time when a visit turned sour and the student did not handle it well.

- The pastor will take each of the students on a hospital or crisis visit before the next session. The pastor should assign the lay person a portion of the visit to oversee. The experience will be discussed at the next session.

Session Evaluation

- Pass out the evaluation form for this session and ask the group to take 3 minutes to fill it in.

- Ask a student to close the session with prayer.

How To Conclude A Sermon Effectively – Leader's Key

The key purpose of a sermon is to persuade, convince, or motivate a person to do something, believe in something, or make some other type of commitment. Therefore, an effective sermon must have a conclusion that <u>invites</u> the congregation to greater belief or to <u>commit</u> to some action. How such an invitation is given will depend on the <u>theme</u> of the sermon, the personality of the <u>preacher</u>, the <u>traditions</u> of the particular church, and the leading of the <u>Spirit</u> in the specific situation.

Some ways to conclude a sermon might include asking the congregation to:

1. Pray a <u>specific</u> prayer or type of prayer. This could be done in the pew, at the altar, or on a kneeling bench.

2. Make a <u>private</u> commitment to God to take some suggested action.

3. Make a private commitment with the <u>minister</u> to take some action suggested by the sermon by raising a hand when only the minister is looking or by handing the minister a note at the end of the service.

4. Make a <u>public</u> commitment to take some action suggested by the sermon by raising a hand, standing, or "coming forward."

5. Fill out a response <u>card</u> which may have a variety of responses and turning that card in to an usher or putting it in the offering.

6. Meet with the minister or other trained person after church in a prayer room or office for further <u>discussion</u>.

7. Take some <u>immediate</u> action that correlates with the <u>sermon</u>, such as taking up an offering or some other action that can be done as a part of the service or immediately after the service.

8. <u>Think</u> about something for a specific period of time and then make a <u>formal</u> commitment of some type at a pre-announced later date.

9. Think about something for an unspecified time and make a <u>personal</u> commitment on their own when the individual is ready.

10. Take part in some additional spiritual <u>discipline</u> that will help them clarify what commitment they may need to make at a later time. Examples of such disciplines might include <u>fasting</u>, tithing or taking part in a deeper level discipleship course to prepare a person for some greater level of commitment that will be made in the future.

You should never attempt to <u>force</u> a person to respond. All you can do is <u>offer</u> the invitation to respond. Forced responses seldom have a <u>lasting</u> impact and may even have a negative impact on the person's overall spiritual journey.

How To Conclude A Sermon Effectively - Student's Worksheet

The key purpose of a sermon is to persuade, convince or motivate a person to do something, believe in something or make some other type of commitment. Therefore, an effective sermon must have a conclusion that _____ the congregation to greater belief or to _____ to some action. How such an invitation is given will depend on the _____ of the sermon, the personality of the _____, the _____ of the particular church and the leading of the _____ in the specific situation.

Some ways to conclude a sermon might include asking the congregation to:

1. Pray a _____ prayer or type of prayer. This could be done in the pew, at the altar, or on a kneeling bench.

2. Make a _____ commitment to God to take some suggested action.

3. Make a private commitment with the _____ to take some action suggested by the sermon by raising a hand when only the minister is looking or handing the minister a note at the end of the service.

4. Make a _____ commitment to take some action suggested by the sermon by raising a hand, standing, or "coming forward."

5. Fill out a response _____ which may have a variety of responses and turning that card in to an usher or putting it in the offering.

6. Meet with the minister or other trained person after church in a prayer room or office for further _____.

7. Take some _____ action that correlates with the _____ such as taking up an offering or some other action that can be done as a part of the service or immediately after the service.

8. _____ about something for a specific period of time and then make a _____ commitment of some type at a pre-announced later date.

9. Think about something for an unspecified time and make a _____ commitment on their own when the individual is ready.

10. Take part in some additional spiritual _____ that will help them clarify what commitment they may need to make at a later time. Examples of such disciplines might include _____, tithing, or taking part in a deeper level discipleship course to prepare a person for some greater level of commitment that will be made in the future.

You should never attempt to _____ a person to respond. All you can do is _____ the invitation to respond. Forced responses seldom have a _____ impact and may even have a negative impact on the person's overall spiritual journey.

How to Handle a Crisis Visit – Leader's Key

Advance Preparation:

1. Prepare your <u>skills</u> by taking whatever crisis <u>training</u> that may be available in your community for issues such as:

a.	Domestic abuse	e. First aid
b.	Suicide intervention	f. Disaster relief
c.	Sexual assault	g. Grief counseling
d.	Violent crimes	

2. Prepare your <u>mind</u> by understanding that people who are feeling overwhelmed with a situation may turn to you because they do not know who else to call. You may not be the person they should have called, but you can be a listening <u>ear</u>. You may need to <u>refer</u> the person to other services in order for the person to receive real help. In most states, <u>clergy</u> are mandated reporters in cases involving the abuse of a minor.

3. Prepare your <u>emotions</u> by being empathetic but not emotionally involved in the situation. Stay <u>focused</u> on your training and think clearly.

During the Crisis:

1. Establish a <u>rapport</u> with the person in crisis.

   A crisis makes someone feel like no one can <u>understand</u> why he or she is upset, which in turn makes him or her more upset. To defeat this <u>cycle</u>, it's important to win the person's trust. Never tell someone in crisis how to <u>feel</u>. Instead <u>validate</u> their feelings by saying something like: "I might feel that way too if I were in your situation." Speak in a calm, even voice, which isn't always easy if someone is angry or screaming.

2. Let the person tell his or her <u>story</u>.

   Be an active <u>listener</u>. Help the person understand that you are really listening by asking <u>questions</u> and/or <u>repeating</u> back what they just said to you. People often feel better if they can tell their story and know they have been heard.

3. Listen for signs of <u>major</u> problems.

   Be alert for certain words and phrases that might indicate a person is in profound distress. Statements such as "This is hopeless" or "My life is over" may be indications of serious danger. If you sense the person may be considering <u>suicide</u>, be very direct. Though this may feel awkward to you, it may save the person's life.

4. Offer <u>hope</u> without misleading the person.

   If it is a situation which you are experienced in, you might say something based on your <u>past</u> experience about the likelihood of a positive outcome. Or if some of the training you have taken has taught you some <u>factual</u> information about the situation, you may offer that information. For example: "I know from past situations that a teenager who says he is going to run away seldom actually does." "When situations like this occur, 90% of the time it is resolved in less than 48 hours." These kinds of statements let the person in crisis know the <u>odds</u> are on their side. But such statements also acknowledge that the situation may not be resolved the way they want it to be. Offer hope, but do not make up stories or statistics that are not factual or that provide a <u>false</u> hope. Otherwise you may cause more harm than good if a <u>worst</u> case scenario happens.

5. Help the person develop an action <u>plan</u>.

   Once you have enough <u>information</u>, you can help the person in crisis explore his or her options, both in the current instance and for the future. It's important to avoid a response that <u>blames</u> the person for what happened. Once the situation is under control, formulate a plan for moving <u>forward</u>. Exploring alternatives and finding a path to a solution helps a person get through the short-term state of a crisis.

After the Crisis:

1. Contact <u>legal</u> authorities or other agencies if required.

2. Make a <u>follow up</u> visit or phone call to the distressed person within 24 hours.

3. Make a <u>record</u> of the situation and how you responded. Keep it on file in case the situation comes up again or you become involved in legalities regarding the crisis.

How to Handle a Crisis Visit – Student Key

Advance Preparation:

1. Prepare your _____ by taking whatever crisis _____ that may be available in your community for issues such as:

    a.   Domestic abuse   e. First aid

    b.   Suicide intervention   f. Disaster relief

    c.   Sexual assault   g. Grief counseling

    d.   Violent crimes

2. Prepare your _____ by understanding that people who are feeling overwhelmed with a situation may turn to you because they do not know who else to call. You may not be the person they should have called, but you can be a listening _____. You may need to _____ the person to other services in order for the person to receive real help. In most states, _____ are mandated reporters in cases involving the abuse of a minor.

3. Prepare your _____ by being empathetic but not emotionally involved in the situation. Stay _____ on your training and think clearly.

During the Crisis:

1. Establish a _____ with the person in crisis.

    A crisis makes someone feel like no one can _____ why he or she is upset, which in turn makes him or her more upset. To defeat this _____, it's important to win the person's trust. Never tell someone in crisis how to _____. Instead _____ their feelings by saying something like: "I might feel that way too if I were in your situation." Speak in a calm, even voice, which isn't always easy if someone is angry or screaming.

2. Let the person tell his or her _____.

    Be an active _____. Help the person understand that you are really listening by asking _____ and/or _____ back what they just said to you. People often feel better if they can tell their story and know they have been heard.

3. Listen for signs of _____ problems.

    Be alert for certain words and phrases that might indicate a person is in profound distress. Statements such as "This is hopeless" or "My life is over" may be indications of serious danger. If you sense the person may be considering _____, be very direct. Though this may feel awkward to you, it may save the person's life.

4. Offer _____ without misleading the person.

    If it is a situation which you are experienced in, you might say something based on your _____ experience about the likelihood of a positive outcome. Or if some of the training you have taken has taught you some _____ information about the situation, you may offer that information. For example: "I know from past situations that a teenager who says he is going to run away seldom actually does." "When situations like this occur, 90% of the time it is resolved in less than 48 hours." These kinds of statements let the person in crisis know the _____ are on their side. But such statements also acknowledge that the situation may not be resolved the way they want it to be. Offer hope, but do not make up stories or statistics that are not factual or that provide a _____ hope. Otherwise you may cause more harm than good if a _____ case scenario happens.

5. Help the person develop an action _____.

    Once you have enough _____, you can help the person in crisis explore his or her options, both in the current instance and for the future. It's important to avoid a response that _____ the person for what happened. Once the situation is under control, build a plan for moving _____. Exploring alternatives and finding a path to a solution helps a person get through the short-term state of a crisis.

After the Crisis:

1. Contact _____ authorities or other agencies if required.

2. Make a _____ visit or phone call to the distressed person within 24 hours.

3. Make a _____ of the situation and how you responded. Keep it on file in case the situation comes up again or you become involved in legalities regarding the crisis.

Role Plays – Crisis Visits: Death and Job Loss

Unlike our other role plays, these two are not pre-written. The reason they are not pre-written is to help demonstrate that the principles of a good visit have actually been comprehended by the learners. Split the students into two groups. Give each group one of the scenarios below. Allow the students five minutes to discuss how they will create a role play based on the scenarios below. The role play itself should last 5-10 minutes.

Model an effective visit to a family who has just experienced an unexpected death. One or two students should play the role of the people making the visit and one or two students should play the role of the members of a family who have just experienced a death.

Model an effective visit to a man who has just lost his job and is facing serious financial repercussions. If there are not enough students, have the pastor role play the person who has just lost his job.

Evaluation Form for Session Four: How to Conclude a Sermon Well and Making Crisis Visits

Please evaluate the session using the scale below.

Completely Agree (5)   Partially Agree (4)   Neither Agree nor Disagree (3)

Partially Disagree (2)   Completely Disagree (1)

Preaching Segment:

The teacher was prepared for the session.

5   4   3   2   1

Time was used effectively during the session.

5   4   3   2   1

I understand why the ending of a sermon is so crucial.

5   4   3   2   1

I see the value in giving an invitation at the end of a sermon.

5   4   3   2   1

I can explain at least two ways to give an invitation at the end of a sermon.

5   4   3   2   1

The most helpful part of this segment was

_____

One suggestion for improving this segment in the future would be

_____

Pastoral Care Segment:

The teacher was prepared for the session.

5   4   3   2   1

Time was used effectively during the session.

5   4   3   2   1

I understand the difference between a crisis visit and other types of pastoral visitation.

5   4   3   2   1

I understand the basics of what I should say when making a crisis visit.

5   4   3   2   1

I see the value of avoiding saying certain things when making a crisis visit.

5   4   3   2   1

I feel that I can be prepared to offer hope in times of crisis.

5   4   3   2   1

The most significant aspect of making a crisis visit is

_____

I feel this way because

_____

The most helpful part of this segment was

_____

One suggestion for improving this segment in the future would be

_____

Practical Application Segment:

The teacher was prepared for the session.

5   4   3   2   1

Time was used effectively during the session.

5   4   3   2   1

The role play about the crisis visit was helpful.

5   4   3   2   1

The sermon preached by my classmate was a helpful example of what we learned in class.

5   4   3   2   1

I understand my assignment for the next session.

5   4   3   2   1

The most helpful part of this segment was

_____

One suggestion for improving this segment in the future is

_____

Chapter 9

How to Use a Sermon Series and How to Avoid a Visitation Disaster

A sermon series is used when the material is too much to be covered in a single sermon. If a lay preacher only has to fill the pulpit from time to time, then each sermon might be independent of the others and the need for using a sermon series may never arise. But when a person becomes part of a pastoral leadership team and begins to preach on a more regular basis, then it at some point that individual will end up either preaching an entire sermon series or preach one sermon in a part of a series that the rest of the team is helping to preach. Therefore understanding the value of using a sermon series is important. This chapter will help a lay preacher think through how to use a sermon series.

No matter how much a person prepares for a visit and no matter how experienced the person may be at making pastoral visits, eventually a visit will go poorly. Sometimes a visit is more than poor, sometimes it turns into a disaster. While visitation disasters should be avoided if at all possible, when they do happen, a person on a pastoral leadership team must know how to respond. A poor response can turn a bad situation into a disastrous one, which may take a tremendous amount of time and energy to repair relationally and spiritually. This chapter will help equip lay people to respond in an emotionally and spiritually mature way to difficult situations that may arise in the course of a pastoral visit.

Session Five Teaching Plan

Welcome and Greeting Time (20 minutes)

- The pastor should ask the students how the week has been and for any special prayer needs.

- The pastor should call on one of the students to open in prayer.

- Review the worksheet "How to Conclude a Sermon" that was used in the last session.

Learning to Preach Segment (1 hour)

- Begin this segment with a 10-minute discussion about the issues facing the communities the lay people live in. Guide that discussion to help the students understand how one sermon alone may not address those issues completely. That insufficiency often leads to the need for a series of sermons. Make the transition to the lecture to follow.

- In advance, ask a fellow pastor to visit the class and be prepared to lead a 10-minute discussion of how that pastor develops ideas for a sermon series. Be ready to offer additional ideas that may need to be covered.

- Lead a discussion on the topic, "Effective Use of a Sermon Series," utilizing the worksheet provided.

- After the lecture, lead a time of discussion so the students can respond to what they have learned.

Take a ten-minute break.

Learning to Make Visits Segment (1 hour)

- Review the principles learned in the last session on how to make a good crisis visit.

- Ask a pre-selected student to share about a time that the student made a visit which the student felt was not handled well. Use that as an introduction to the next segment.

- Use the handout to lead a discussion entitled "How to Avoid a Visitation Disaster." Use some recent news stories as illustrations of such disasters. Use the worksheet "What to do if Something Goes Wrong" to lead a discussion of what to do when a visitation disaster occurs. Suggest that for further study, the students might want to purchase Nancy Gorsuch's book, *Pastoral Visitation*.

- After the lesson, ask the class to respond to what they heard.

- End this session with a brief discussion about the legal issues surrounding pastoral malpractice and liability. Feel free to invite a guest speaker to lead this portion of the training.

Take a ten-minute break.

Practical Application Segment (30 minutes)

- Call for oral reports from the visits that were made by the lay people since the last session. How did the visit go? What did the lay people learn? How did the pastor feel having the lay people lead part of the visit?

- "You Want Me to Do What!" role play – have two students read the pre-written role play about an unrealistic expectation a parishioner has for a pastoral visit.

- Role play evaluation: Discuss the role play and how it made the students feel.

- One-point mini-sermon: Ask the pre-selected student to preach the sample sermon.

- Sermon evaluation: lead an evaluation of the sermon, reminding everyone of the purpose of such evaluations.

Assignments for the next session

- Ask for a volunteer to preach a one-point fifteen-minute sermon at the next session. It needs to be someone other than the person who preached at today's session.

- Before the next session, the pastor will take each of the students on one of the three types of visits that have been studied. The lay people should lead the entire visit, with the pastor silently observing. They should reflect on the experience before the next class and be ready to share what they have learned at the next session.

- Ask the class to think how they might be able to work as a team in preaching and pastoral care and be ready to share their ideas in the next session.

Session Evaluation

- Pass out the evaluation form for this session and ask the group to take three minutes to fill it in.

- Ask a student to close the session with prayer.

Effective Use of a Sermon Series – Leader's Key

1. While some texts and topics can be adequately dealt with in a "stand alone" sermon, other texts and issues are better suited for a sermon series. A sermon series allows you to delve deeper into a text or subject than a stand alone sermon. When using more than one preacher in a series, it is important to plan in advance which preacher will cover which texts.

2. A series can be as short as three sermons or as long as eight. Less than three is just not enough to make a real series. More than eight is probably too long for people to connect all the parts to the whole.

3. A series should have an overall theme. Each sermon will address some aspect of that theme. For maximum effectiveness, some sort of review will be necessary to connect the individual sermons to the whole series. Handouts tend to help the series be more effective because it provides a written summary of the entire series after it is completed. If the series would interest the community, it can be used as an outreach tool.

4. Creating a strong series of sermons is a lot of work. It is easy to question the validity of all that work once the series is over, especially if you did not see immediate results from the series. However, a sermon series can continue to be useful long after all the sermons have been preached.

Ways to use a sermon series after it is complete:

- Use CDs/DVDs of the series to give to visitors as a welcome gift.

- Use CDs/DVDs of the series as an outreach tool to the community.

- Use CDs/DVDs to build a "library" of the church's teaching on a particular <u>subject</u>. This is especially helpful to <u>new</u> members who want to know what the church believes on specific issues.

- Distribute CDs/DVDs to those who have become <u>homebound</u> temporarily.

- Use the series to provide <u>theological</u> training to others.

- Convert the sermon series into a weekend <u>seminar</u> or weeklong <u>revival</u> so it can be used again.

Effective Use of a Sermon Series – Student's Worksheet

1. While some texts and topics can be adequately dealt with in a "_____" sermon, other texts and issues are better suited for a _____. A sermon series allows you to delve _____ into a text or subject than a stand alone sermon. When using more than one _____ in a series, it is important to plan in _____ which preacher will cover which texts.

2. A series can be as short as three sermons or as long as _____. Less than three is just not enough to make a real series. More than eight is probably too _____ for people to _____ all the parts to the whole.

3. A series should have an overall _____. Each sermon will address some _____ of that theme. For maximum effectiveness, some sort of review will be necessary to connect the _____ sermons to the whole series. _____ tend to help the series be more effective because it provides a written _____ of the entire series after it is completed. If the series would interest the _____, it can be used as an _____ tool.

4. Creating a _____ series of sermons is a lot of work. It is easy to question the _____ of all that _____ once the series is over, especially if you did not see immediate _____ from the series. However, a sermon series can continue to be _____ long after all the sermons have been preached.

Ways to use a sermon series after it is complete:

- Use CDs/DVDs of the series to give to _____ as a welcome gift.

- Use CDs/DVDs of the series as an _____ tool to the community.

- Use CDs/DVDs to build a "library" of the church's teaching on a particular _____. This is especially helpful to _____ members who want to know what the church believes on specific issues.

- Distribute CDs/DVDs to those who have become _____ temporarily.

- Use the series to provide _____ training to others.

- Convert the sermon series into a weekend _____ or weeklong _____ so it can be used again.

How to Avoid a Visitation Disaster – Leader's Key

1. Know the <u>situation</u> before you go.

2. Phone in advance to state the <u>purpose</u> of the visit.

3. <u>Pray</u>.

4. <u>Refuse</u> to be drawn into an <u>argument</u> or <u>gossip</u> session.

5. Take your <u>Bible</u> and other appropriate <u>literature</u>. If things begin to turn bad, you can open the Bible and read as a way to stop the flow of <u>negativity</u>.

6. Arrive on <u>time</u>. Being early or late creates <u>tension</u>.

7. Take <u>someone</u> with you. This is <u>vital</u> if you are visiting the home of a person of the <u>opposite</u> sex or a minor.

8. Accept but don't expect <u>hospitality</u>. Otherwise you might <u>offend</u> the person.

9. <u>Introduce</u> yourself to those present whom you don't know so that you don't come off as <u>rude</u> or aloof.

10. Take care of your <u>personal</u> needs before the visit (bathroom, drink, etc.).

11. Be non-judgmental in all <u>situations</u>, but don't imply <u>affirmation</u> of all things.

12. Know your <u>limitations</u>. Don't <u>intentionally</u> get into situations you are not equipped to handle. Capitalize on your <u>strengths</u>. This is why you are working as a team with your pastor and other church leaders. You are <u>good</u> at something, so focus on what you are good at.

13. Build visitation times into your <u>weekly</u> schedule. Otherwise, more <u>time</u> may elapse than you realize and that creates <u>hard</u> feelings. A disciplined time for visitation leads to productivity and successful time management.

Adapted from:

Pastoral Visitation by Nancy J. Gorsuch, Augsburg Fortress, Minneapolis, 1999, pages 70-73.

Roger Loomis, http://ministrydirect.com/pastoral_care, accessed October 21, 2008.

What to do if Something Goes Wrong – Leader's Key

1. Stay as <u>calm</u> as possible. <u>Trust</u> the <u>Holy Spirit</u> to get you through the situation.

2. Make a <u>written</u> record as soon as possible after the visit while you still remember the <u>details</u>.

3. Talk to your <u>pastor</u> or other appropriate leadership to apprise them of the situation.

4. Be prepared to <u>admit</u> and <u>correct</u> any part you played in creating the negative situation.

5. Pray for the <u>grace</u> and <u>mercy</u> of God to be upon the situation.

6. Make a follow up <u>contact</u> in a timely way to help remove <u>relational</u> barriers.

Adapted from:

Pastoral Visitation by Nancy J. Gorsuch, Augsburg Fortress, Minneapolis, 1999, pages 70-73.

Roger Loomis, http://ministrydirect.com/pastoral_care, accessed October 21, 2008.

How to Avoid a Visitation Disaster – Student's Worksheet

1. Know the _____ before you go.

2. Phone in advance to state the _____ of the visit.

3. _____.

4. _____ to be drawn into an _____ or _____ session.

5. Take your _____ and other appropriate _____. If things begin to turn bad you can open the Bible and read as a way to stop the flow of _____.

6. Arrive on _____. Being early or late creates _____.

7. Take _____ with you. This is _____ if you are visiting the home of a person of the _____ sex or a minor.

8. Accept but don't expect _____. Otherwise, you might _____ the person.

9. _____ yourself to those present whom you don't know so you don't come off as _____ or aloof.

10. Take care of your _____ needs before the visit (bathroom, drink, etc.).

11. Be non-judgmental in all _____, but don't imply _____ of all things.

12. Know your _____. Don't _____ get into situations you are not equipped to handle. Capitalize on your _____. This is why you are working as a team with your pastor and other church leaders. You are _____ at something, so focus on what you are good at.

13. Build visitation times into your _____ schedule. Otherwise, more _____ may elapse than you realize and that creates _____ feelings. A disciplined time for visitation leads to productivity and successful time management.

Adapted from:

Pastoral Visitation by Nancy J. Gorsuch, Augsburg Fortress, Minneapolis, 1999, pages 70-73.

Roger Loomis, http://ministrydirect.com/pastoral_care, accessed October 21, 2008.

What to do if Something Goes Wrong – Student's Worksheet

1. Stay as _____ as possible. _____ the _____ to get you through the situation.

2. Make a _____ record as soon as possible after the visit while you still remember the _____.

3. Talk to your _____ or other appropriate leadership to apprise them of the situation.

4. Be prepared to _____ and _____ any part you played in creating the negative situation.

5. Pray for the _____ and _____ of God to be upon the situation.

6. Make a follow up _____ in a timely way to help remove _____ barriers.

Adapted from:

Pastoral Visitation by Nancy J. Gorsuch, Augsburg Fortress, Minneapolis, 1999, pages 70-73.

Roger Loomis, http://ministrydirect.com/pastoral_care, accessed October 21, 2008.

Role Play – You Want Me To Do What!

Member: Pastor, did you know that I am having some serious medical treatments tomorrow?

Pastor: No, Sister Exaggeration, I didn't even know you were even sick.

Member: Yes, I am having my toe nail removed. It's been infected for nearly a week.

Pastor: Oh, I didn't know. I'm so sorry.

Member: Well, I wondered why you didn't come by to see me, or send flowers, or bring a meal. Why I've been hurting all week long with no support from you or anyone else.

Pastor: I'm so sorry. No one told me.

Member: Well, of course no one told you; we are not a gossiping church. But if you would visit each person in the church each week to check on them, then you'd know about our needs.

Pastor: Sister Exaggeration, it's hard for me to visit when I'm working down at the factory full time.

Member: I know. You always bring that up. I still think if you had more faith you would quit working at the factory and just trust God to provide for you.

Pastor: I know you feel that way, Sister Exaggeration; you've mentioned it before.

Member: I just think the pastor ought to be totally devoted to God, and working at the factory keeps you from being as devoted as I think you ought to be.

Pastor: I know Sister Exaggeration, but with the church only paying me $75 a week, it's really hard to buy groceries for my family of 5, not to mention the rent and the utilities and gas for the car.

Member: If you were a real man of prayer, God would provide those things for you.

Pastor: God has provided them, through my job at the factory.

Member: Yes, but since you are working there, you won't be able to come sit with me all day when I have my toe nail removed. And you didn't have time to cut the grass for Mrs. Lazy last week when she went on vacation. And you didn't have time to take a meal to Brother Fatz last month when he got the hiccups. And you never even bothered to show up to my second cousin's step sister's best friend's funeral. It really hurt me to think that you didn't have time to comfort me in such a time of personal loss.

Pastor: I know, Sister Exaggeration. I don't think I have ever met all your expectations. I just do the best I can with the time God gives me.

Member: Well, I just wish we had a real pastor. Maybe one day our church can grow and we'll be able to hire a pastor that has time for his congregation.

Pastor: Sister Exaggeration, maybe someday you will be able to hire a real pastor who will have time for you. But in the meantime, you are stuck with me. I'll try to do better and find time to come by tomorrow and visit you when you have your toe nail removed.

Evaluation Form for Session Five: How to Use a Sermon Series and How to Avoid a Visitation Disaster

Please evaluate the session using the scale below.

Completely Agree (5)   Partially Agree (4)   Neither Agree nor Disagree (3)

Partially Disagree (2)   Completely Disagree (1)

Preaching Segment:

The teacher was prepared for the session.

5   4   3   2   1

Time was used effectively during the session.

5   4   3   2   1

I see the value of preaching through a sermon series.

5   4   3   2   1

It makes sense to me that in certain situations a sermon series would be more helpful.

5   4   3   2   1

I have confidence that I can learn how to plan out a sermon series.

5   4   3   2   1

Two places I can find ideas for planning out a sermon series are

_____

These places will be helpful to me because

_____

The most helpful part of this segment was

_____

One suggestion for improving this segment in the future would be

_____

Pastoral Care Segment:

The teacher was prepared for the session.

5   4   3   2   1

Time was used effectively during the session.

5   4   3   2   1

I realize the inherent dangers of pastoral visitation.

5   4   3   2   1

I understand why I need to decide in advance how I will respond to these dangers.

5   4   3   2   1

I can think of two ways to avoid a visitation disaster.

5   4   3   2   1

The visitation disaster I fear most personally is

_____

I feel this way because

_____

The most helpful part of this segment was

_____

One suggestion for improving this segment in the future would be

_____

Practical Application Segment:

The teacher was prepared for the session.

5   4   3   2   1

Time was used effectively during the session.

5   4   3   2   1

The role play about the visitation disasters was helpful.

5   4   3   2   1

The sermon preached by my classmate was a helpful example of what we learned in class.

5   4   3   2   1

I understand my assignment for the next session.

5   4   3   2   1

The most helpful part of this segment was

_____

One suggestion for improving this segment in the future is

_____

Chapter 10

Creating Pastoral Ministry Teams
to Improve Preaching and Visitation

As this training process draws to a close, it is important to help the group develop a plan for how to continue the process of working together as a pastoral leadership team. No training process will ever be able to cover every aspect of how such a team might look in an individual church or what subjects they may need to address that are unique to that church. But through prayer, discussion and a commitment to team work, a pastoral leadership team can develop and help the church become more effective. This chapter will help the pastor and lay people think through both the theological and practical implications of the importance of such teams. Much of the material in this chapter comes from the first two chapters of this book. It is assumed that the pastor will have read those two chapters in their entirety before teaching the course. While it is hoped that the students may have also read those two chapters, this chapter has been written specifically so that the students can complete this course without having read those two chapters. The excerpts used here could also be shared with the entire church as a part of helping the church understand the value of this process. This chapter has been designed to make such sharing more practical.

Session Six Teaching Plan

Welcome and Greeting Time (10 minutes)

- The pastor should ask the students how the week has been and for any special prayer needs.

- The pastor should call on one of the students to open in prayer.

Theological and Theoretical Foundations for Creating Pastoral Leadership Teams (1 ½ hours)

- Use the worksheet to review the biblical foundation for multiple leaders in the local church.

- Use the worksheet to discuss the current realities of bivocational ministry.

- Use the worksheet to discuss how to create pastoral leadership teams in the local church.

- Lead a guided discussion about the importance of ensuring the continuity of doctrine when using multiple preachers.

- Lead a discussion about the importance of long term planning when using a team approach.

- Lead a brief brainstorming session regarding special days (ie: Christmas, Easter, Mother's Day, Church Anniversaries, etc.) in the life of a church and the expectations people may have for who preaches on those days.

Take a ten-minute break.

Learning to Make Visits Segment (20 minutes)
- Lead a discussion on the importance of keeping the rest of the team informed when using a team approach to pastoral visitation.

- Discuss the importance of maintaining confidentiality and how it contrasts with keeping other team members informed.

Practical Application Segment (1 hour)
- Call for oral reports from the visits that were made by the lay people since the last session. How did the visits work out? What did the lay people learn? How did the pastor feel about having the lay people lead the visits?

- One-point mini-sermon: Ask the preselected student to preach the sample sermon.

- Sermon evaluation: lead a time of evaluation of the sermon, reminding everyone of the purpose of such evaluations.

- Assign each student a date to preach during the Sunday morning worship service over the next three–five weeks. Remind them to have three-five key lay leaders in the church use the Church Sermon Assessment Tool (appendix F) to help them evaluate the sermon. If those lay leaders need any explanation about using the assessment tool, the pastor should provide those instructions when distributing the assessment tool. The pastor and the lay preacher should meet a day or two after the sermon is delivered and review the Church Sermon Assessment Tool and make suggestions for improvement.

- The pastor will work with other pastors, or denominational leaders, to coordinate a date for the lay people to preach in nearby churches, perhaps a week or two after preaching in the home church. The same assessment tool will be used.

- Concluding remarks and discussion of any future plans for additional training.

Session Evaluation

- Pass out the evaluation form for this session and ask the group to take three minutes to fill it in.

- Ask a student to close the session with prayer.

Biblical Foundations for Multiple Leaders in the Church – Leader's Key

Introduction

Building effective pastoral <u>leadership</u> teams requires having a thorough knowledge of the theology of church leadership. Attempts to build these teams based on <u>human</u> organizational principles or modern <u>business</u> methodology will be inadequate in properly preparing lay people to work together in the spiritual dynamic of pastoral leadership teams.

Bivocational Ministry Is Normative for the Church

The New Testament reflects bivocational ministry as <u>normative</u> for the church. This does not mean that <u>every</u> pastor in the New Testament was bivocational or even that it is the <u>preferred</u> style of pastorate. But it is important to remember that a large number of New Testament churches were led by bivocational pastors. Modern church attendees have come to expect pastors to devote all of their <u>time</u> to the ministries of the church and to not work an outside job. The members of modern churches must understand that it is <u>normal</u> to have pastors who work additional jobs and are therefore unable to be <u>personally</u> involved in every aspect of church life. These members must come to accept the necessity of having <u>multiple</u> leaders in the church who work together to meet the needs of the church instead of expecting the <u>pastor</u> to do it all.

The following scriptures demonstrate the normalcy of bivocational ministry: Acts 18:1-4, 1 Thessalonians 2:9, 2 Thessalonians 3:7-9

The transition away from bivocational ministry came as a result of the desire of churches to have a more <u>educated</u> clergy. "In an attempt to raise the educational level of our ministerial leadership, churches and denominations in this country established a number of colleges and seminaries. <u>Professionalism</u> came with education."[97]

Though all ministers should strive to be professionals, <u>seminary</u> education alone is not a guarantee of such behavior. This is especially true if a person's call to ministry came <u>later</u> in life and the individual is already a professional in another field.

Shared Pastoral Leadership Is Normative for the Church

The New Testament demonstrates a <u>shared</u> pastoral leadership model as normative for the church. In modern times, many North American Protestant churches have become accustomed to a <u>single</u> pastor model of church leadership. The single pastor is often expected to do almost all of the <u>preaching</u> and pastoral care.

When the bulk of the preaching and pastoral care is <u>centered</u> on one person, it creates the impression that this individual has more <u>authority</u> than the New Testament gives the pastor. Once the congregation perceives that the pastor has all the authority, it follows that the pastor also bears all the <u>responsibility</u> for getting everything done. The church expects the pastor to provide most of the <u>leadership</u> and manpower in the church as well as accept most of the <u>blame</u> for any faults in the church. An example of multiple leadership can be found in Acts 13:1-3. When pastors find themselves in churches that do not have multiple leaders, <u>developing</u> leaders should be one of the first priorities. The biblical precedent for this is found in 2 Timothy 2:1-2.

Multiple Callings to Ministry Exist in a Healthy Church

The New Testament teaches that there are <u>multiple</u> callings to ministry and that all of them are needed for a <u>healthy</u> church.[98] God calls all Christians to serve Him in a <u>general</u> sense as followers of Christ.[99]

God also calls certain people to a <u>deeper</u> level of service to the church.[100] Those people who have been called to a deeper level of service should be working together as a <u>team</u> to make sure all the ministries of the church are accomplished effectively.

The <u>terms</u> used to identify individuals who respond to God's call are varied. Common terms include: elders, pastors, preachers, messengers of the Word, deacons, bishops, overseers, evangelists and apostles. "The terminology is not as important as is the clear biblical model of teamwork needed to <u>govern</u> the local church."[101]

Alexander Strauch, a noted authority on the subject of biblical leadership, writes, "Whatever terminology you choose to describe local church leaders will have advantages and disadvantages. In the end, every local church is responsible to teach its people the <u>meaning</u> of the terms it uses to describe its spiritual leaders, whether it be elders, overseers, ministers, preachers, or pastors."[102] Whatever titles are given to these multiple leaders is less important than the fact that there should be a <u>plurality</u> of people who are working together as teams to lead churches. A key passage that demonstrates different callings in ministry is 1 Timothy 5:17.

The Local Church Is the Primary Training Experience for Ministry

Modern church attendees have placed so great an emphasis on <u>formal</u> theological training that they have missed the role the <u>church</u> was designed to fill in training people for ministry. In the New Testament, the <u>local</u> church was the <u>primary</u> training experience for ministry. In order to build effective pastoral leadership teams, the church must once again become the preeminent place for ministry <u>training</u>. That is not to say that formal <u>theological</u> training has no value and should not be pursued. It simply means that when such training occurs in <u>isolation</u> from the local church, it has significantly less <u>value</u> than church-based training.

What frequently happens when individuals express a call to <u>vocational</u> ministry is that they are encouraged to go <u>away</u> to seminaries to learn how to fulfill their calling. When they graduate, churches <u>hire</u> them to serve as pastoral leaders. This is very different than how people were <u>trained</u> in the New Testament. "The early church did not recruit elders from a distant seminary."[103]

But most of the <u>leaders</u> of the New Testament church were trained on the job as they <u>served</u> alongside other leaders.[104] The local church was the <u>primary</u> training experience for ministry. 2 Timothy 2:1-2 clearly speaks to this issue.

Conclusion

The modern North American church has forgotten its <u>history</u> and theology of church leadership. As the church rediscovers that <u>bivocational</u> ministry is normal, it will help remove some of the stigma that is often associated with bivocational ministry. As the church rediscovers that <u>shared</u> pastoral leadership is both biblical and more emotionally <u>healthy</u> for the pastors, it will remove significant pressure from pastors serving in single leadership situations. As the church rediscovers the importance of all its members knowing and fulfilling various types of callings to <u>ministry</u>, key people will emerge who can help provide <u>team</u> leadership to the church. As the church rediscovers its own role in <u>training</u> people for ministry, such ministerial training will be more church-based and therefore more practical and beneficial to the church. With a better understanding of these theological principles, pastors and churches can examine the practical realities of applying these theological principles to their unique situations.

Biblical Foundations for Multiple Leaders in
the Church - Student's Worksheet

Introduction

Building effective pastoral _____ teams requires having a thorough knowledge of the theology of church leadership. Attempts to build these teams based on _____ organizational principles or modern _____ methodology will be inadequate in properly preparing people to work together in the spiritual dynamic of pastoral leadership teams.

Bivocational Ministry Is Normative for the Church

The New Testament reflects bivocational ministry as _____ for the church. This does not mean that _____ pastor in the New Testament was bivocational or even that it is the _____ style of pastorate. But it is important to remember that a large number of New Testament churches were led by bivocational pastors. Modern church attendees have come to expect pastors to devote all of their _____ to the ministries of the church and not work an outside job. The members of modern churches must understand that it is _____ to have pastors who work additional jobs and are therefore unable to be _____ involved in every aspect of church life. These members must come to accept the necessity of having _____ leaders in the church who work together to meet the needs of the church instead of expecting the _____ to do it all.

The following scriptures demonstrate the normalcy of bivocational ministry: Acts 18:1-4, 1 Thessalonians 2:9, 2 Thessalonians 3:7-9

The transition away from bivocational ministry came as a result of the desire of churches to have a more _____ clergy. "In an attempt to raise the educational level of our ministerial leadership, churches and denominations in this country established a number of colleges and seminaries. _____ came with education."[105] Though all ministers should strive to be professionals, _____ education alone is not a guarantee of such behavior. This is especially true if a person's call to ministry came _____ in life and the individual is already a professional in another field.

Shared Pastoral Leadership Is Normative for the Church

The New Testament demonstrates a _____ pastoral leadership model as normative for the church. In modern times, many North American Protestant churches have become accustomed to a _____ pastor model of church leadership. The single pastor is often expected to do almost all of the _____ and pastoral care.

When the bulk of the preaching and pastoral care is _____ on one person, it creates the impression that this individual has more _____ than the New Testament gives the pastor. Once the congregation perceives that the pastor has all the authority, it follows that the pastor also bears all the _____ for getting everything done. The church expects them to provide most of the _____ and manpower in the church as well as accept most of the _____ for any faults in the church. An example of multiple leadership can be found in Acts 13:1-3.

When pastors find themselves in churches that do not have multiple leaders, _____ leaders should be one of the first priorities. The biblical precedent for this is found in 2 Timothy 2:1-2.

Multiple Callings to Ministry Exist in a Healthy Church

The New Testament teaches that there are _____ callings to ministry and that all of them are needed for a _____ church.[106] God calls all Christians to serve Him in a _____ sense as followers of Christ.[107] God also calls certain people to a _____ level of service to the church.[108] Those people who have been called to a deeper level of service should be working together as a _____ to make sure all the ministries of the church are accomplished effectively.

The _____ used to identify individuals who respond to God's call are varied. Common terms include: elders, pastors, preachers, messengers of the Word, deacons, bishops, overseers, evangelists and apostles. "The terminology is not as important as is the clear biblical model of teamwork needed to _____ the local church."[109] Alexander Strauch, a noted authority on the subject of biblical leadership, writes, "Whatever terminology you choose to describe local church leaders will have advantages and disadvantages. In the end, every local church is responsible to teach its people the _____ of the terms it uses to describe its spiritual leaders, whether it be elders, overseers, ministers, preachers, or pastors."[110] Whatever titles are given to these multiple leaders is less important than the fact that there should be a _____ of people who are working together as teams to lead churches.

A key passage that demonstrates different callings in ministry is 1 Timothy 5:17.

The Local Church Is the Primary Training Experience for Ministry

Modern church attendees have placed so great an emphasis on _____ theological training that they have missed the role the _____ was designed to fill in training people for ministry. In the New Testament, the _____ church was the _____ training experience for ministry. In order to build effective pastoral leadership teams, the church must once again become the preeminent place for ministry _____. That is not to say that formal _____ training has no value and should not be pursued. It simply means that when such training occurs in _____ from the local church, it has significantly less _____ than church-based training.

What frequently happens when individuals express a call to _____ ministry is that they are encouraged to go _____ to seminaries to learn how to fulfill their calling. When they graduate, churches _____ them to serve as pastoral leaders. This is very different than how people were _____ in the New Testament. "The early church did not recruit elders from a distant seminary."[111]

But most of the _____ of the New Testament church were trained on the job as they _____ alongside other leaders.[112]

The local church was the _____ training experience for ministry. 2 Timothy 2:1-2 clearly speaks to this issue.

Conclusion

The modern North American church has forgotten its _____ and theology of church leadership. As the church rediscovers that _____ ministry is normal, it will help remove some of the negative stigma that is often associated with bivocational ministry. As the church rediscovers that _____ pastoral leadership is both biblical and more emotionally _____ for the pastors, it will remove significant pressure from pastors serving in single leadership situations. As the church rediscovers the importance of all its members knowing and fulfilling various types of callings to _____, key people will emerge who can help provide _____ leadership to the church. As the church rediscovers its own role in _____ people for ministry, such ministerial training will be more church-based and therefore more practical and beneficial to the church. With a better understanding of these theological principles, pastors and churches can examine the practical realities of applying these theological principles to their unique situations.

Realities of Bivocational Ministry – Leader's Key

There are a number of current cultural trends to understand regarding bivocational ministry.

Bivocational Ministry Is Becoming More Common

Bivocational ministry is becoming more <u>common</u> in North American Protestant churches. Regardless of how pastors and/or church attendees may feel about bivocational ministry, it is a <u>growing</u> practice in North American church life. "The majority of congregations in the United States are small, with fewer than <u>100</u> regular members, and cannot typically afford their own pastor."[113] This results in a <u>growing</u> need for more bivocational pastors every year.

Patricia Chang, research professor at Boston College, has studied several denominations and written extensively about clergy issues. Her findings demonstrate that "the current religious landscape is skewed towards a very <u>large</u> number of <u>small</u> congregations and a <u>small</u> number of <u>large</u> congregations."[114] Most of those small congregations will be unable to fully-fund their pastors, which will result in those churches seeking bivocational pastors to guide them.

Bivocational pastors do not need to have <u>negative</u> feelings about their status. Dennis Bickers reminds the bivocational pastors that he works with to "never let the misconceptions others may have about your ministry cause you to question your <u>call</u> and your <u>value</u> to the work of the kingdom of God."[115] Bivocational pastors are not second class ministers. They are a <u>growing</u> segment of American church life.

Experience Burn-out if They Do Not Delegate

A second trend that is important to understand is the increasing number of pastors experiencing <u>burn-out</u>. A 2002 article in *Pulpit and Pew* discovered that "doctrinal and theological differences aside, North American churches have in common not only the Cross and a love of Christ, but also a pastorate whose <u>health</u> is fast becoming cause for concern."[116]

Many factors contribute to this lack of health. One of the factors that lead to burn-out is <u>loneliness</u>. When pastors do not feel they have anyone to <u>share</u> their burdens with, they feel isolated and alone. Loneliness can lead to <u>depression</u>. When pastors feel depressed, they are more vulnerable to emotional <u>fatigue</u>, to the practice of unhealthy <u>habits</u> and to increased levels of <u>anxiety</u>. Therefore, systems must be put in place to help pastors overcome feelings of depression so they can be healthier individuals and more effective in their ministries. When such systems are not in place, pastors become trapped in a downward <u>spiral</u> that feeds upon itself until they become emotionally <u>paralyzed</u> in ministry and in their personal lives.

A second factor that leads to burnout is the general <u>brokenness</u> of modern society which brings additional challenges to pastors who are seeking to bring healing to their communities. H. B. London, of Focus on the Family, writes, "Today's pastors face crises unknown to any other occupational groups. Contemporary parish ministry, without anyone intending to make it so, has become an emotional and spiritual H-bomb, ready to <u>explode</u> any second."[117] Loneliness, depression, a compulsion to fix society, and the internal politics of local churches combine together to make pastoral ministry a <u>difficult</u> calling to fulfill.

While all pastors face the same challenges, "bivocational pastors usually face those challenges with less formal education, training, and resources, but that does not mean they are doomed to be defeated."[118] As bivocational pastors are taught how to build pastoral leadership teams, they will be less prone to feelings of loneliness. As bivocational pastors learn to share the burdens of ministry with an entire team, they will no longer feel as overwhelmed.

Building pastoral leadership teams requires a willingness to delegate some duties to others. Delegation, the lifeline many ministers must grasp in order to avoid burn-out, will be a challenge for some bivocational pastors to practice. Bivocational pastors must learn to resist the temptation to work themselves to exhaustion. Exhaustion will quickly lead to burnout.

Delegating menial tasks may be easier to do, but for delegation to really help, pastors must also be willing to delegate some of the preaching and pastoral care duties. Because these are two of the most time consuming and emotionally draining aspects of ministry, a failure to delegate a portion of these duties will result in pastors still not having time to rest. "It is a highly significant but often overlooked fact that our Lord did not appoint one man to lead His church. He personally appointed and trained twelve men."[119] These were not twelve men whom helped with menial tasks but men who Jesus sent out to preach, teach and address the needs of people. Pastors need to follow the example of Jesus and recruit help in their preaching and pastoral care efforts. As pastors learn to give away part of their ministry to others, they will have less stress. Less stress will help them avoid burn-out and stay in their ministry positions longer.

Lay People Can and Will Help if Trained Effectively

A third key trend is the willingness of the laity to work in greater partnership with the clergy. Common thought among many ministry leaders is that the laity does not want to be involved in church work. Pastors must help the laity accept more responsibility. Pastors must learn to let go of their own need to be in control. Pastors need to address their desires to personally solve all the problems in the church.

While many people would agree that lay people can effectively lead in certain areas of ministry, they may not feel as confident that lay people can preach and accomplish pastoral care duties effectively. However, with the right encouragement and training, individuals in the church can be taught how to deliver an effective sermon and do basic pastoral care. Not only can they be taught this, but many people are willing to do these things if they are trained properly.

Formal Theological Education Is Helpful but Not Necessary

The final trend to recognize is that while a formal theological education is helpful, it is not necessary for a person to accomplish effective ministry. Some church and/or denominational leaders may feel that teaching lay people to preach and giving them significant pastoral duties will weaken the church. The underlying idea of many denominational leaders is that lay people cannot preach as well as seminary trained professional clergy. It is important to remember that when God calls people to serve Him, God will help those people answer that calling regardless of the level of their formal theological education.

Conclusion

When pastors come to understand these four trends, they will be ready to embark on the journey of discovering, enlisting, training, and releasing their pastoral leadership teams for effective ministry.

Realities of Bivocational Ministry – Student's Worksheet

There are a number of current cultural trends to understand regarding bivocational ministry.

Bivocational Ministry Is Becoming More Common

Bivocational ministry is becoming more _____ in North American Protestant churches. Regardless of how pastors and/or church attendees may feel about bivocational ministry, it is a _____ practice in North American church life. "The majority of congregations in the United States are small, with fewer than _____ regular members, and cannot typically afford their own pastor."[120] This results in a _____ need for more bivocational pastors every year.

Patricia Chang, research professor at Boston College, has studied several denominations and written extensively about clergy issues. Her findings demonstrate that "the current religious landscape is skewed towards a very _____ number of _____ congregations and a _____ number of _____ congregations."[121] Most of those small congregations will be unable to fully-fund their pastors, which will result in those churches seeking bivocational pastors to guide them.

Bivocational pastors do not need to have _____ feelings about their status. Dennis Bickers reminds the bivocational pastors that he works with to "never let the misconceptions others may have about your ministry cause you to question your _____ and your _____ to the work of the kingdom of God."[122] Bivocational pastors are not second class ministers. They are a _____ segment of American church life.

Pastors Experience Burn-out if They Do Not Delegate

A second trend that is important to understand is the increasing number of pastors experiencing _____. A 2002 article in *Pulpit and Pew* discovered that "doctrinal and theological differences aside, North American churches have in common not only the Cross and a love of Christ, but also a pastorate whose _____ is fast becoming cause for concern."[123]

Many factors contribute to this lack of health. One of the factors that leads to burn-out is _____. When pastors do not feel they have anyone to _____ their burdens with, they feel isolated and alone. Loneliness can lead to _____. When pastors feel depressed, they are more vulnerable to emotional _____, to the practice of unhealthy _____ and to increased levels of _____. Therefore, systems must be put in place to help pastors overcome feelings of depression so they can be healthier individuals and more effective in their ministries. When such systems are not in place, pastors become trapped in a downward _____ that feeds upon itself until they become emotionally _____ in ministry and in their personal lives.

A second factor that leads to burnout is the general _____ of modern society which brings additional challenges to pastors who are seeking to bring healing to their communities. H. B. London, of Focus on the Family, writes, "Today's pastors face crises unknown to any other occupational groups. Contemporary parish ministry, without anyone intending to make it so, has become an emotional and spiritual H-bomb, ready to _____ any second."[124] Loneliness, depression, a compulsion to fix society, and the internal politics of local churches combine together to make pastoral ministry a _____ calling to fulfill.

While all pastors face the same challenges, "bivocational pastors usually face those challenges with less _____ education, training, and resources, but that does not mean they are doomed to be defeated."[125] As bivocational pastors are taught how to build pastoral leadership _____, they will be less prone to feelings of loneliness. As bivocational pastors learn to share the _____ of ministry with an entire team, they will no longer feel as overwhelmed.

Building pastoral leadership teams requires a willingness to _____ some duties to others. Delegation, the lifeline many ministers must grasp in order to avoid burn-out, will be a _____ for some bivocational pastors to practice. Bivocational pastors must learn to resist the temptation to work themselves to _____. Exhaustion will quickly lead to burnout.

Delegating menial tasks may be easier to do, but for delegation to really help, pastors must also be willing to delegate some of the _____ and pastoral _____ duties. Because these are two of the most time consuming and emotionally draining aspects of ministry, a failure to delegate a portion of these duties will result in pastors still not having time to rest. "It is a highly significant but often overlooked fact that our Lord did not appoint one man to lead His church. He personally appointed and trained _____ men."[126]

These were not twelve men whom helped with _____ tasks but men who Jesus sent out to preach, teach and address the needs of people. Pastors need to follow the example of Jesus and _____ help in their preaching and pastoral care efforts. As pastors learn to give away part of their _____ to others, they will have less stress. Less _____ will help them avoid burn-out and stay in their ministry positions longer.

Lay People Can and Will Help if Trained Effectively

A third key trend is the willingness of the laity to work in greater _____ with the clergy. Common thought among many ministry leaders is that the laity does not want to be _____ in church work. Pastors must help the laity accept more _____. Pastors must learn to let go of their own need to be in control. Pastors need to address their desires to personally _____ all the problems in the church.

While many people would agree that lay people can effectively lead in certain areas of ministry, they may not feel as confident that lay people can _____ and accomplish pastoral _____ duties effectively. However, with the right encouragement and _____, individuals in the church can be taught how to deliver an _____ sermon and do basic pastoral care. Not only can they be taught this, but many people are willing to do these things if they are trained properly.

Formal Theological Education Is Helpful but Not Necessary

The final trend to recognize is that while a formal theological education is _____, it is not necessary for a person to accomplish effective ministry. Some church and/or denominational leaders may feel that teaching lay people to preach and giving them significant pastoral duties will

_____ the church. The underlying idea of many denominational leaders is that lay people cannot preach as well as seminary trained _____ clergy. It is important to remember that when God _____ people to serve Him, God will _____ those people answer that calling regardless of the level of their formal theological education.

Conclusion

When pastors come to understand these four trends, they will be ready to embark on the journey of discovering, enlisting, training, and releasing their pastoral leadership teams for effective ministry.

Proposal for Creating a Pastoral Leadership Team – Leader's Key

1. Pray and seek the <u>will</u> of God to determine if this is the right <u>style</u> of leadership to pursue for your specific church.

2. Spend three to six <u>months</u> teaching the congregation <u>why</u> this leadership style would be right for your church. Consider teaching chapters 1-3 of this book to the entire <u>congregation</u> over a period of time.

3. Ask the congregation to "<u>test</u>" out this leadership style for one year before actually making any changes to the church constitution or bylaws.

4. Ask the congregation to <u>set</u> <u>aside</u> those individuals who will be a part of the pastoral leadership team. <u>Elect</u> them to this team if that is what your congregational polity calls for.

5. Create a <u>preaching</u> <u>schedule</u> that includes each person on the team. The schedule can be any system that works for your team, but a suggestion would be that the pastor preaches three Sundays a month and one of the other people from the team preaches one Sunday a month. In a month that has five Sundays, a second person from the team would preach one time.

6. Create a <u>pastoral</u> <u>care</u> schedule that includes each person on the team. This can take a variety of forms, such as splitting the entire congregation up into groups with each team member assigned a group, giving each team member one week a month to do whatever visitation needs to be done, having the team members make any visits that arise on the pastor's day off or when out of town, or having one week a month when the pastor makes no visits and the rest of the team makes all the visits. The goal is to give the pastor a break in order to avoid burn-out. Any system that meets that goal will be a success.

7. Meet once a <u>month</u> to <u>plan</u> sermon topics and update each other on who received a visit and who still needs one.

8. <u>Spend</u> a day together once a <u>year</u> to plan the major annual focuses of the church.

Proposal for Creating a Pastoral Leadership Team-Student's Worksheet

1. Pray and seek the _____ of God to determine if this is the right _____ of leadership to pursue for your specific church.

2. Spend three to six _____ teaching the congregation _____ this leadership style would be right for your church. Consider teaching chapters 1-3 of this book to the entire _____ over a period of time.

3. Ask the congregation to "_____" out this leadership style for one year before actually making any changes to the church constitution or bylaws.

4. Ask the congregation to _____ those individuals who will be a part of the pastoral leadership team. _____ them to this team if that is what your congregational polity calls for.

5. Create a _____ that includes each person on the team. The schedule can be any system that works for your team, but a suggestion would be that the pastor preaches three Sundays a month and one of the other people from the team preaches one Sunday a month. In a month that has five Sundays, a second person from the team would preach one time.

6. Create a _____ schedule that includes each person on the team. This can take a variety of forms, such as splitting the entire congregation up into groups with each team member assigned a group, giving each team member one week a month to do whatever visitation needs to be done, having the team members make any visits that arise on the pastor's day off or when he is out of town, or having one week a month when the pastor makes no visits and the rest of the team makes all the visits. The goal is to give the pastor a break so that he does not burn-out. Any system that meets that goal will be a success.

7. Meet once a _____ to _____ sermon topics and update each other on who received a visit and who still needs one.

8. _____ a day together once a _____ to plan the major annual focuses of the year of the church.

Evaluation Form for Session Six: Creating Pastoral Ministry Teams to Improve Preaching and Visitation

Please evaluate the session using the scale below.

Completely Agree (5)   Partially Agree (4)   Neither Agree nor Disagree (3)

Partially Disagree (2)   Completely Disagree (1)

Preaching Segment:

The teacher was prepared for the session.

5   4   3   2   1

Time was used effectively during the session.

5   4   3   2   1

It is possible to ensure the continuity of doctrine when using multiple preachers.

5   4   3   2   1

I can explain to someone else the importance of long term planning when using a team approach.

5   4   3   2   1

I realize that special events will have to be dealt with in appropriate ways.

5   4   3   2   1

My greatest concern in becoming a part of a pastoral leadership team is

_____

I believe this because

_____

The most helpful part of this segment was

_____

One suggestion for improving this segment in the future would be

_____

Pastoral Care Segment:

The teacher was prepared for the session.

5   4   3   2   1

Time was used effectively during the session.

5   4   3   2   1

I understand the importance of keeping the pastoral leadership team informed of visits.

5   4   3   2   1

I see the value of keeping confidentiality after making a pastoral visit.

5   4   3   2   1

What excites me the most about working with a pastoral leadership team is

_____

I feel this way because

_____

The most helpful part of this segment was

_____

One suggestion for improving this segment in the future would be

_____

Practical Application Segment:

The teacher was prepared for the session.

5   4   3   2   1

Time was used effectively during the session.

5   4   3   2   1

The sermon preached by my classmate was a helpful example of what we learned in class.

5   4   3   2   1

The discussion about how to implement plural pastoral leadership in my church was helpful.

5   4   3   2   1

The most helpful part of this segment was

_____

One suggestion for improving this segment in the future is

_____

Appendix A

Training Course Overview

For distribution to interested laypeople

Every year godly pastors who serve small churches will leave the ministry because they are required to work second jobs and simply cannot endure the pressure. Some of these pastors will eventually re-enter the ministry, but many will never return to a calling they once found so fulfilling. While there are many reasons why such pastors may leave the ministry, a significant one is that they simply burn-out. The pressure of working secular jobs and carrying on the duties of leading churches become too great for some bivocational pastors to bear. When these pastors leave the ministry, the churches are deprived of their experience, their passion, and their unique gifts and talents. Churches cannot afford to continue to lose so many good pastors.

While some churches will eventually grow and be able to fully-fund pastors, many churches will remain relatively small because of the communities they are located in. But such communities desperately need those small churches and those small churches desperately need good pastors. While it may be unrealistic to expect small churches to fully-fund pastors, it is not unrealistic to ask churches to consider creating systems in which both the churches, and the pastors who serve them, are healthy.

The New Testament contains leadership principles to help churches form pastoral leadership teams to assist pastors in the preaching and pastoral care of the church. Some members of the congregation may not be interested in serving on a pastoral leadership team. But those who are interested are invited to take part in a six week training process. For more information, contact _____.

Further details, including an outline for the six sessions, will be sent out to those lay people who express interest in taking part.

Appendix B

Syllabus for Developing Leadership Teams in the Bivocational Church

Each of the six sessions will have three 55-minute segments with a short break in between each segment. Ideally the sessions will happen weekly or bi-weekly.

I. Session One: Introduction to Preaching and Pastoral Care

    A. Learning to Preach Segment:

        1. Why Should We Preach?

        2. What Should We Preach?

        3. How Should We Preach?

    B. Learning to Make Visits Segment:

        1. Why Should We Visit?

        2. Who Should We Visit?

        3. How Should We Visit?

    C. Practical Application Segment:

        1. "Pastor Is Going Out of Town" role play

        2. "The Worst Visit Ever" role play

        3. Assignments for the next session

        4. Session evaluation

II. Session Two: Selecting the Sermon Text and Making Hospital Visits

    A. Learning to Preach Segment:

        1. How do I select a text?

        2. How do I study the text?

    B. Learning to Make Visits Segment:

        1. Overview of how to make an effective hospital visit

        2. What do I say?

        3. What do I avoid saying?

        4. How do I end the visit?

    C. Practical Application Segment:

    1. "Hospital Visit" role play

    2. Role play evaluation

    3. Assignments for the next session

    4. Session evaluation

III. Session Three: Strengthening Sermon Preparation, Presenting the Sermon and Making Absentee Visits

    A. Learning to Preach Segment:

        1. How do I present a sermon?

        2. Why are some methods easier to use than others?

        3. How can I learn how to use methods I am not as familiar with?

    B. Learning to Make Visits Segment:

        1. Overview of how to make an effective absentee visit

        2. What do I say?

        3. What do I avoid saying?

        4. How do I end the visit?

    C. Practical Application Segment:

        1. "Absentee Visit" role play

        2. Role play evaluation

        3. One point mini-sermon

4. Sermon evaluation

5. Assignments for the next session

6. Session evaluation

IV. Session Four: How to Conclude a Sermon Well and Making Crisis Visits

    A. Learning to Preach Segment:

        1. Why is the ending so important?

        2. How do I give an invitation?

        3. Practical suggestions for small churches

    B. Learning to Make Visits Segment:

        1. Overview of how to make an effective crisis visit

        2. What do I say?

        3. What do I avoid saying?

        4. How do I end the visit?

    C. Practical Application Segment:

        1. "Crisis Visit" role play

        2. Role play evaluation

        3. One point mini-sermon

        4. Sermon evaluation

        5. Assignments for the next session

        6. Session evaluation

V. Session Five: How to Use a Sermon Series and How to Avoid a Visitation Disaster

    A. Learning to Preach Segment:

        1. Why use a sermon series?

        2. When do I not use a sermon series?

        3. Where do I find ideas for a sermon series?

    B. Learning to Make Visits Segment:

        1. How do I avoid visitation disasters?

        2. What do I do if I sense a visitation disaster approaching?

3. What should I do if a visitation disaster happens?

4. Legal issues regarding visitation disasters

C. Practical Application Segment:

1. "You Want Me to Do What!" role play

2. Role play evaluation

3. One point mini-sermon

4. Sermon evaluation

5. Assignments for the next session

6. Session evaluation

VI. Session Six: Creating Pastoral Ministry Teams to Improve Preaching and Visitation

A. Theological and Theoretical Foundations for Creating Pastoral Leadership Teams

1. Ensuring continuity of doctrine and comprehension when using multiple preachers

2. The importance of long-term planning

3. What about "special days"?

B. Learning to Make Visits Segment:

1. Keeping the rest of the team informed

2. Maintaining confidentiality

C. Practical Application Segment:

1. One point mini-sermon

2. Sermon evaluation

3. Discussion of how plural pastoral leadership might work in the context of your local church

4. Session evaluation

5. Concluding remarks and discussion of any future plans

Appendix C

Peer Evaluation Form for Visitation Role Plays

Please answer these statements using the following scale:

Completely Agree (5)   Partially Agree (4)   Neither Agree nor Disagree (3)

Partially Disagree (2)   Completely Disagree (1)

The purpose of the visit was clearly expressed.

5   4   3   2   1

Comments: _____

The scriptures were used effectively during the visit.

5   4   3   2   1

Comments: _____

Prayer was used effectively during the visit.

5   4   3   2   1

Comments: _____

The principles of an effective visit were evident.

5   4   3   2   1

Comments: _____

The body language matched the words being used.

5   4   3   2   1

Comments: _____

What was the most helpful idea you gained from this role play?

What is one suggestion for improvement in this skill you would like to offer your classmate?

Appendix D

Evaluation Form for Student Mini-Sermons

In order to help develop your classmate's preaching skills, please mark this evaluation form using the scale below.

Excellent (5)   Very good (4)   Good (3)   Average (2)   Needs Improvement (1)

If you mark a one (needs improvement), please write a suggestion for how to improve next to it.

Effective Use of Scripture

Scripture used was appropriate to theme of sermon.

5   4   3   2   1

Scripture was read with expression and clarity.

5   4   3   2   1

The main point flowed naturally from the scripture passage.

5   4   3   2   1

The scripture passage was adequately explained.

5   4   3   2   1

Effective Delivery Style

The introduction got my attention.

5   4   3   2   1

The introduction laid the foundation for the sermon.

5   4   3   2   1

The speaker spoke with confidence and conviction.

5   4   3   2   1

The speaker's voice, inflection, and volume were appropriate.

5   4   3   2   1

The speaker's gestures and facial expressions were appropriate.

5   4   3   2   1

The speaker made eye contact with the audience.

5   4   3   2   1

Life Application

The sermon would touch a real need in most congregations.

5   4   3   2   1

The sermon dealt with contemporary issues.

5   4   3   2   1

The sermon made the connection between the biblical world and modern culture.

5   4   3   2   1

In a church setting, the sermon would be helpful to both Christians and non-Christians.

5   4   3   2   1

This sermon would have moved many church attendees.

5   4   3   2   1

Sermon Conclusion

The sermon conclusion adequately wrapped up the points that were made.

5   4   3   2   1

The purpose of the sermon was made clear.

5   4   3   2   1

I was challenged to think or do something specific as a result of the sermon.

5   4   3   2   1

General Issues

The length of the sermon was appropriate.

5   4   3   2   1

The illustrations used seemed to support the points.

5   4   3   2   1

The speaker appeared honest.

5   4   3   2   1

The speaker's personal appearance was not distracting.

5   4   3   2   1

The speaker made adequate use of available technology.

5   4   3   2   1

Appendix E

Pastoral Visit Evaluation Form

The pastor should fill out this form and discuss it with the person being trained in how to make pastoral visits.

Please use the following scale to complete this form.

Completely Agree (5)   Partially Agree (4)   Neither Agree nor Disagree (3)

Partially Disagree (2)   Completely Disagree (1)

The purpose of the visit was made clear.

5   4   3   2   1

Scripture was used effectively.

5   4   3   2   1

Prayer was used effectively.

5   4   3   2   1

Adequate concern was shown for the person being visited.

5   4   3   2   1

The length of the visit was appropriate.

5   4   3   2   1

The most significant moment of the visit was

_____

A part of the visit that could have used improvement was

_____

Church Sermon Assessment Tool

In order to help develop our guest speaker's preaching skills, please mark this evaluation form using the scale below.

Excellent (5)   Very good (4)   Good (3)   Average (2)   Needs Improvement (1)

If you mark a one (needs improvement), please write a suggestion for how to improve next to it.

Effective Use of Scripture

Scripture used was appropriate to theme of sermon.

5   4   3   2   1

Scripture was read with expression and clarity.

5   4   3   2   1

The main points flowed naturally from the scripture passage.

5   4   3   2   1

The scripture passage was adequately explained.

5   4   3   2   1

Effective Delivery Style

The introduction got my attention.

5   4   3   2   1

The introduction laid the foundation for the sermon.

5   4   3   2   1

The speaker spoke with confidence and conviction.

5   4   3   2   1

The speaker's voice, inflection and volume were appropriate.

5   4   3   2   1

The speaker's gestures and facial expressions were appropriate.

5   4   3   2   1

The speaker made eye contact with the audience.

5   4   3   2   1

Life Application

The sermon touched a real need in my life.

5   4   3   2   1

The sermon dealt with contemporary issues.

5   4   3   2   1

The sermon made the connection between the biblical world and modern culture.

5   4   3   2   1

The sermon was equally helpful to both Christians and non-Christians.

5   4   3   2   1

I was moved by this sermon.

5   4   3   2   1

Sermon Conclusion

The conclusion adequately wrapped up the points that were made.

5   4   3   2   1

The purpose of the sermon was made clear.

5   4   3   2   1

I was challenged to think or do something specific as a result of the sermon.

5   4   3   2   1

General Issues

The length of the sermon was appropriate.

5   4   3   2   1

The illustrations used seemed to support the points.

5   4   3   2   1

The speaker appeared honest.

5   4   3   2   1

The speaker's personal appearance was not distracting.

5   4   3   2   1

The speaker made adequate use of available technology.

5   4   3   2   1

End Notes

1. Dennis W. Bickers, *The Tentmaking Pastor: The Joy of Bivocational Ministry* (Grand Rapids: Baker Books, 2000), 10.

2. Doran C. McCarty, "Reflections on Bivocational Ministry? In *Meeting the Challenge of Bivocational Ministry: A Bivocational Reader*, ed. Doran C. McCarty (Nashville: Seminary Extension, 1996), 7.

3. Southern Baptist Bivocational Minister's Association, *Bivocational Ministry*, http:www. sbbma.org/Bivocational%20Ministry.pdf, accessed May 7. 2008.

4. Dennis Bickers, The Work of the Bivocational Minister (Valley Forge: Judson Press, 2007), 3.

5. Ronald Hornecker and Doran C. McCarty, *Making the Most of Change* (St. Augustine: McCarty Library, 1998), 95.

6. Steve Nerger, *Bivocational Church Planters: Uniquely Wired for Kingdom Growth* (Alpharetta: North America Mission Board, 2007), 4.

7. Bickers, *The Work of the Bivocational Pastor*, 6.

8. SBC Executive Committee, *Meet Southern Baptists* (Nashville: SBC Executive Committee, 2005), 3.

9. Merwyn Borders, *The Circle Comes Full: New England Southern Baptists, 1958-1998* (Franklin: Providence House Publishers, 1998), 93.

10. Southern Baptist Directory Services, *Summary of ACP Statistics,* http://sbds.lifeway.com/Reports/f93530_115445.htm, accessed May 12, 2008.

11. Adelle M. Banks, *Mississippi Most Religious, Vermont Least*, http://www.usatoday.com/news/religion/2009-01-29-faith-state-survey_N.htm, accessed December 11, 2009.

12. Sybil Brigham McShane, *Mobile Library Literacy: Solutions for a Rural Environment,* http://www.firstmonday.org/issues/issue6_4/mcshane/index.html, accessed May 6, 2008.

13. Melvin J. Steinbron, *Can the Pastor Do It Alone?* (Eugene: Wipf and Stock Publishers, 2004), 58.

14. Roy W. Trueblood and Jackie B. Trueblood, *Partners in Ministry: Clergy and Laity* (Nashville: Abingdon Press, 1999), 93.

15. Ron Rice, "Encouraging a Shared Ministry Plan through the Development and Implementation of a Bivocational Ministry Covenant" (D. Min. diss., Golden Gate Baptist Theological Seminary, 1998), 25.

16. Bickers, *The Work of the Bivocational Minister*, 14.

17. English Standard Version, ESV.

18. F. F. Bruce, *The Book of the Acts, Revised*, The New International Commentary on the New Testament, ed. Gordon D. Fee (Grand Rapids: Eerdmans Publishing Company, 1988), 346.

19. Darrell L. Bock, *Acts*, Baker Exegetical Commentary on the New Testament, eds. Robert W. Yarbrough and Robert H. Stein (Grand Rapids: Baker Academic, 2007), 578.

20. Bickers, *The Tentmaking Pastor: The Joy of Bivocational Ministry*, 103.

21. Holman Christian Standard Version, HCSB.

22. Gene L. Green, *The Letters to the Thessalonians*, The Pillar New Testament Commentary, ed. D. A. Carson (Grand Rapids: Eerdmans, 2002), 129.

23. Ibid., 90.

24. Ibid., 131.

25. New Living Translation, NLT.

26. Green, *The Letters to the Thessalonians*, 346.

27. 1 Tim. 5:9-15.

28. Green, *The Letters to the Thessalonians*, 346.

29. James Greene, *The Dual Career Minister: Bivocational Ministry in the 21st Century* (Cary: Baptist State Convention of North Carolina, 1989), 7.

30. Bickers, *The Work of the Bivocational Minister*, 14.

31. Greene, *The Dual Career Ministry: Bivocational Ministry in the 21st Century*, 7.

32. Luther M. Dorr, *The Bivocational Pastor* (Nashville: Broadman Press, 1988), 102-103.

33. Ibid., 96.

34. George Barna, *Today's Pastors* (Ventura: Regal Books, 1993), 82.

35. Larry Kreider, Ron May, Steve Prokopchak, Brian Sauder, *The Biblical Role of Elders for Today's Church: New Testament Leadership Principles for Equipping Elders* (Ephrata: House to House Publications, 2004), 81.

36. English Standard Version, ESV.

37. Bock, *Acts*, 439.

38. Kreider, et al., *The Biblical Role of Elders for Today's Church: New Testament Leadership Principles for Equipping Elders*, 11.

39. Bruce, *The Books of the Acts, Revised*, 246.

40. New Living Translation, NLT.

41. Philip H. Towner, *The Letters to Timothy and Titus*, The New International Commentary on the New Testament, ed. Gordon D. Fee (Grand Rapids: Eerdmans Publishing Company, 2006), 491.

42. Rom. 12:3-8; 1 Cor. 12:4-11.

43. Eph. 4:1-7.

44. Mark 3:14-19.

45. Roy W. Trueblood and Jackie B. Trueblood, *Partners in Ministry: Clergy and Laity*, 80.

46. 1 Tim. 4:14.

47. Matt Willmington, *Am I Called to Ministry?* http://willimington.wordpress.com/2008/02/12/aim-i-called-to-ministry, accessed May 13, 2008.

48. Ibid.

49. Kreider, et al., *The Biblical Role of Elders for Today's Church: New Testament Leadership Principles for Equipping Elders*, viii.

50. Alexander Strauch, *Biblical Eldership: An Urgent Call to Restore Biblical Church Leadership* (Littleton: Lewis and Roth Publishers, 1995), 33.

51. New Living Translation, NLT.

52. Towner, *The Letters to Timothy and Titus*, 361.

53. 1 Tim. 3:2.

54. Raymond F. Collins, *1 and 2 Timothy and Titus*, The New Testament Library, eds. C. Clifton Black, John T. Carroll and Beverly Roberts Gaventa (Louisville: Westminster John Knox Press, 2002), 144.

55. Ibid., 145.

56. New Living Translation, (NLT).

57. Kreider, et al., *The Biblical Role of Elders for Today's Church: New Testament Leadership Principles for Equipping Elders*, 3.

58. Ibid., 16.

59. Acts 20.

60. Susan Willhauck, "Cultivating a Culture of the Call: A Model for Lay Theological Education," *Theological Education* 38, No. 2 (November 2002): 113.

61. Ibid., 113.

62. Barbara J. Fleischer, "The Ministering Community as Context for Religious Education: A Case Study of St. Gabriel's Catholic Parish," *Religious Education* 10, No. 1 (Winter 2006): 105.

63. Holman Christian Standard Version, (HCSV).

64. Collins, *1 and 2 Timothy and Titus*, 318.

65. Ibid., 326.

66. Towner, *The Letters to Timothy and Titus*, 693.

67. Dennis Bickers, *The Bivocational Pastor: Two Jobs, One Ministry* (Kansas City: Beacon Hill Press, 2004) 28.

68. Patricia M. Y. Chang, *Assessing the Clergy Supply in the 21st Century*, http:www.pulpitandpew.duke.edu/chang.html, accessed May 8, 2008.

69. Linda Lawson, *Tentmaking Ministers Predicted to Become Southern Baptist Norm*, http://bpnews.net/bpnews.asp=373, accessed May 7, 2008.

70. Southern Baptist Bivocational Minister's Association, *Bivocational Ministry*, http://www.sbna.org/Bivocational%20Ministry.pdf, accessed May 8, 2008.

71. Lifeway Research, *SBC Totals – 1971-2006*, http://www.lifeway.com/lwcI_research_chart_SBC_Totals_1971-2006.jpg, accessed May 8. 2008.

72. Chang, *Assessing the Clergy Supply in the 21st Century*, accessed May 8, 2008.

73. Bickers, *The Tentmaking Pastor: The Joy of Bivocational Ministry*, 40.

74. Bob Wells, *Which Way to Clergy Health?*, http://www.pulpitandpew.duke.edu/clergyhealth.html, accessed May 15, 2008.

75. Bickers, *The Tentmaking Pastor: The Joy of Bivocational Ministry*, 25.

76. Fred Lehr, *Clergy Burnout: Recovering from the 70-Hour Work Week . . . and Other Self-Defeating Practices* (Minneapolis: Fortress Press, 2006), 45.

77. Wells, *Which Way to Clergy Health?*, accessed May 15, 2008.

78. H. B. London, Jr. and Neil B. Wiseman, *Your Pastor is an Endangered Species* (Wheaton: Victor Books, 1996), 15.

79. Bickers, *The Tentmaking Pastor: The Joy of Bivocational Ministry*, 59.

80. Bickers, *The Work of the Bivocational Minister*, 9.

81. Bickers, *The Tentmaking Pastor: The Joy of Bivocational Ministry*, 45.

82. Phil A. Newton, *Elders in Congregational Life: Rediscovering that Biblical Model for Church Leadership* (Grand Rapids: Kregal Publications, 2005), 119.

83. Alexander Strauch, *Biblical Eldership: An Urgent Call to Restore Biblical Church Leadership* (Littleton: Lewis and Roth Publishers, 1995), 33.

84. George Barna, *Today's Pastors* (Ventura: Regal Books, 1993), 36.

85. Ibid., 37.

86. H. B. London, Jr. and Neil B. Wiseman, *Your Pastor is an Endangered Species*, 15.

87. Lehr, *Clergy Burnout*, 45.

88. Bickers, *The Work of the Bivocational Minister*, 85.

89. Ibid., 85.

90. Bickers, *The Bivocational Pastor: Two Jobs, One Ministry*, 119.

91. Kreider et al., *The Biblical Role of Elders for Today's Church: New Testament Leadership Principles for Equipping Elders*, 196.

92. Barna, *Today's Pastors*, 157.

93. Craig Boehlke, "Lay Preaching: A Mixed Bag," *Word and World* 24, no. 3 (2004) : 333.

94. Kreider et al., *The Biblical Role of Elders for Today's Church: New Testament Leadership Principles for Equipping Elders*, 16.

95. Nerger, *Bivocational Church Planters, Uniquely Wired for Kingdom Growth*, 13.

96. Diane Melbye, "Lay Preaching: A Blessed Necessity," *Word and World* 24, no. 3 (2004) : 330.

97. Greene, *The Dual Career Ministry: Bivocational Ministry in the 21ˢᵗ Century*, 7.

98. Romans 12:3-8; 1 Corinthians 12:4-11.

99. Ephesians 4:1-7.

100. Mark 3:14-19.

101. Kreider et al., *The Biblical Role of Elders for Today's Church: New Testament Leadership Principles for Equipping Elders*, viii.

102. Alexander Strauch, *Biblical Eldership: An Urgent Call to Restore Biblical Church Leadership* (Littleton: Lewis and Roth Publishers, 1995), 33.

103. Kreider, et al., *The Biblical Role of Elders for Today's Church: New Testament Leadership Principles for Equipping Elders*, 11.

104. Acts 20.

105. Greene, *The Dual Career Ministry: Bivocational Ministry in the 21ˢᵗ Century*, 7.

106. Romans 12:3-8; 1 Corinthians 12:4-11.

107. Ephesians 4:1-7.

108. Mark 3:14-19.

109. Kreider et al., *The Biblical Role of Elders for Today's Church: New Testament Leadership Principles for Equipping Elders*, viii.

110. Alexander Strauch, *Biblical Eldership: An Urgent Call to Restore Biblical Church Leadership* (Littleton: Lewis and Roth Publishers, 1995), 33.

111. Kreider et al., *The Biblical Role of Elders for Today's Church: New Testament Leadership Principles for Equipping Elders*, 16.

112. Acts 20.

113. Patricia M. Y. Chang, *Assessing the Clergy Supply in the 21ˢᵗ Century*, http:www.pulpitandpew. duke.edu/chang.html, accessed May 8, 2008.

114. Ibid.

115. Bickers, *The Tentmaking Pastor: The Joy of Bivocational Ministry*, 40.

116. Bob Wells, *Which Way to Clergy Health?*, http://www.pulpitandpew.duke.edu/clergyhealth. html, accessed May 15, 2008.

117. H. B. London, Jr. and Neil B. Wiseman, *Your Pastor is an Endangered Species* (Wheaton: Victor Books, 1996), 15.

118. Bickers, *The Tentmaking Pastor: The Joy of Bivocational Ministry*, 59.

119. Alexander Strauch, *Biblical Eldership – Restoring the Eldership to Its Rightful Place in the Church, Revised* (Littleton: Lewis and Roth Publishers, 1997), 12.

120. Patricia M. Y. Chang, *Assessing the Clergy Supply in the 21ˢᵗ Century*, http:www.pulpitandpew. duke.edu/chang.html, accessed May 8, 2008.

121. Ibid.

122. Bickers, *The Tentmaking Pastor: The Joy of Bivocational Ministry*, 40.

123. Bob Wells, *Which Way to Clergy Health?*, http://www.pulpitandpew.duke.edu/clergyhealth. html, accessed May 15, 2008.

124. H. B. London, Jr. and Neil B. Wiseman, *Your Pastor is an Endangered Species* (Wheaton: Victor Books, 1996), 15.

125. Bickers, *The Tentmaking Pastor: The Joy of Bivocational Ministry*, 59.

126. Alexander Strauch, *Biblical Eldership – Restoring the Eldership to Its Rightful Place in the Church, Revised* (Littleton: Lewis and Roth Publishers, 1997), 12.

Breinigsville, PA USA
25 August 2010
244131BV00002B/1/P